Truth Announced

Preaching That Persuades
Preaching With Parables
Preaching to the Heart
Communicating with 20th Century Man
Sense Appeal and Storytelling

Jay E. Adams

Institute for Nouthetic Studies, a ministry of Mid-America Baptist Theological Seminary, Arlington, TN
mabts.edu and nouthetic.org

Truth Announced by Jay E. Adams
Copyright © 2026 by the Institute for Nouthetic Studies,

Preaching That Persuades © 2007
Preaching with Parables © 2007
Preaching to the Heart © 1983
Communicating with 20th Century Man © 1979

New Testament quotations are from the Christian Counselor's New Testament and Proverbs Copyright © 2019 by the Institute for Nouthetic Studies. © 1977, 1980, 1994, 2000 by Jay E. Adams

ISBN: 978-1-949737-91-2 (Print)
ISBN: 978-1-949737-92-9 (eBook)

Editor: Donn R. Arms

Library of Congress Cataloging-in-Publication Data
Names: Adams, Jay E., 1929 - 2020
Title: Truth Announced
Jay E. Adams
Description: Arlington: Institute for Nouthetic Studies, 2026
Identifiers: ISBN 9781949737912 (paper)
Classification: LCC BV4211.2.A325| DDC 251

All rights reserved. No part of this publication may be reproduced, stored in a retrieval system, or transmitted in any form or by any means – electronic, mechanical, photocopy, recording, or any other – except for brief quotations in printed reviews, without prior permission of the publisher.

Published in the United States of America

Foreword by the Editor

It is a joy to publish *Truth Announced*, a second collection of essays on preaching by Jay Adams. The first volume, *Truth Apparent*, is a collection of shorter essays Dr. Adams wrote for two journals for which he was a regular contributor. The third volume in this series is entitled *Truth Applied*.

This volume consists of four monographs and a chapter he contributed to a book on preaching. The titles of each section are self-explanatory, and Dr. Adams explains them in his introductions to each better than I could here. But let me say a word about his essay *Communicating with 20th Century Man*. Do not let his reference to "20th Century Man" tempt you to overlook this chapter, thinking it to be too outdated to be of help. While he makes several references to life as it was in 1979 when he penned this article, the principles he explains are timeless. "20th Century Man" was simply the peg upon which he hung his thoughts. I considered renaming his essay *Communicating with Modern Man,* but, as with all Dr. Adams' books we republish, we have kept the editing to a minimum, desiring to let Dr. Adams' voice be heard clearly for generations to come who never had the opportunity to meet him or hear him preach.

Both experienced preachers and students just beginning to preach will profit from these essays. Each speaks to an important aspect of the great work to which God has called you.

Donn R Arms, ed.

*It was revealed to them
that they were serving not themselves
but you,
in the things that have now been announced to you
through those who preached the good news to you
by the Holy Spirit sent from heaven,
things into which angels long to look.
1 Peter 1:12*

Contents

Preaching That Persuades

Introduction	
1 - The Preacher's Language Must Be Biblical	1
2 - A Case In Point	6
3 - Clarity	9
4 - Confrontation	16
5 - Contemporaneity	20
6 - Conviction	24
7 - Concern	28
8 - Concreteness	34
9 - Conversation	39
10 - Conciseness	43
11 - Conclusion	47

Preaching with Parables

Introduction	51
1 - From Proverb to Parable	53
2 - What the Word Tells Us	55
3 - A Special Sort of Story	57
4 - Let's Take One Apart	60
5 - Becoming a Good Scribe	65
6 - About Proverbs	68
7 - Features to Recognize	71
8 - Let's Begin	74
9 - Shaping Up	78
10 - When and Where to Use Parables	82

11 - Placing the Parable	85
12 - How to Do It	87
13 - Internal Parables	90
14 - Parables and Illustrations	93
15 - Practice in Expanding Proverbs	95
16 - Practice in Extending Proverbs	98
Conclusion	102

Preaching to the Heart

Introduction	105
1 - What Is the Heart?	107
2 - Two Kinds of Hearts	111
3 - Preaching From the Heart	115
4 - Boldness of the Heart	119
5 - Preaching From God's Heart	125
6 - Heart-Convicting Preaching	129
7 - A Heart-Adapted Form	134
Conclusion	137

Communicating With 20th Century Man

1 - The Signs of the Times	142
2 - Knowing and Going	154
3 - Form and Substance	161
4 - Do It Well	171

Sense Appeal and Storytelling

Sense Appeal and Storytelling	183

PREACHING THAT PERSUADES

Introduction

In Proverbs we read that a person's "sweetness of lips [speech] increases persuasiveness" (Proverbs 16:21), that "the wise of heart uses his mouth prudently, and to his lips he adds persuasion" (v. 23), and that "pleasant words flowing with honey are sweetness to the soul and healing to the bones" (v. 24). Obviously, in these verses the writer is advising all believers about their speech, not just those who proclaim God's truth. But if what he says is true of the speech of every Christian, how much more should it be true of the minister of the Word whose stock-in-trade is speech?

Those whose hearts contain wisdom, he says, use their mouths "prudently." What does that mean? Prudent speech is speech in which one takes care about what he says and how he says it. It is speech, as the passage says, that comes from inner wisdom.[1] Consequently, this speech seems "sweet" (convincing) to those who hear and thus persuades them.

The "sweetness" of speech describes the way in which one perceives what he hears. To him it is as sweet as honey.[2] Now, in our society, we often speak of those who use honeyed words as covering some ulterior intention. But that was not what Solomon meant by the image. Such speech he considers desirable, wholesome—something to be diligently cultivated, because it is right and, therefore, persuasive.

Does that mean that we must soften harsh facts? Not at all. But what it does mean is that, harsh or otherwise, what we say ought to strike the listener as persuasive because it is wise in content, style, and application. All of us at some point have failed to convince others, not from a lack of facts but from a failure to present them convincingly. That is what I am deeply concerned to help the reader of this volume to cultivate: speech that will persuade because it is entirely appropriate to the persons he teaches.

---

1   The Hebrew word *bin* as it is used here means balanced, considered, weighed speech that leads to wise judgments.
2   Honey was the universal sweetener in Mediterranean lands; they did not use sugar as we do. To this day, I eat baklava—a honey desert—at my favorite Greek restaurant.

Chapter One

The Preacher's Language Must Be Biblical

The preacher must learn to use the language of the Holy Spirit. In describing his own preaching Paul wrote, "It is these things about which we speak, not in words taught by human wisdom[1] but in those that are taught by the Spirit, combining spiritual teaching with spiritual words" (1 Corinthians 2:13). Here, Paul refers to the fact that his preaching was inspired by the Spirit Who gave him the wisdom to speak prudently.[2]

Using Spiritual Language

"But," you say, "we are not inspired. How can we use the Holy Spirit's words?"

The answer is that we learn what sort of speech the Holy Spirit utilized and requires of us by studying the preaching of Jesus, the apostles, and the prophets. Naturally, we shall find this exclusively in the Scriptures.

"That may be true, but does that mean we may not speak any other words than those found on the pages of the Bible?"

Of course not. That isn't what I mean. Biblical preaching interprets Scripture and applies it to those who listen. To do this, we must employ the words of our own language in ways that make the message clear and persuasive. Calvin asked, "For what ought sermons and doctrines be except expositions of what Scripture contains? Truly, if we add the slightest nuance, it only results in corruption."[3] But it is not only the content of the apostolic message that we should replicate; it is also the "words" in which that message was communicated by the apostles. We must focus on their language.

---

1 N.B., Once more we see that proper speech is connected with wisdom. That wisdom, Paul says, is from God.
2 I cannot develop the fact that apostolic preaching, according to Christ's prediction, was inspired. Here, that fact must be assumed. For a detailed discussion of the matter see my book *Preaching According to the Holy Spirit*.
3 John Calvin, *Sermons on the Book of Micah*, Benjamin W. Farley, trans. and ed. P&R Pub. Co., Phillipsburg (2002), p. 160.

In other words, we must learn from what they said under the influence of the Holy Spirit and attempt to duplicate in our language and context what they did in theirs. They set forth the pattern by which we discover what "spiritual" (Spirit-given) language is like. We should study it intensively in order to understand and follow that pattern.

Two Characteristics of Biblical Language

Biblical language is "wholesome." That vivid description may seem strange to you, but it is decidedly a major concern of God's. Listen to what Paul said when writing to Timothy:

> *Teach and urge these things. Whoever teaches differently and doesn't agree with the wholesome words of our Lord Jesus Christ and the teaching that is in keeping with godliness, is conceited, understands nothing. He has an unhealthy desire for discussions and controversies over words, from which come envy, strife, blasphemies, suspicions, evils, incessant wranglings ... (1 Timothy 6:2c-5a).*

The attitudes of such people are obviously wrong. But it is not only their attitudes; it is also how they handle words that is in question. Their "controversies over words" and their failure to agree with Christ's "wholesome words" give us a clear indication that wholesomeness of speech (or healthy speech) is critical to the proper proclamation of the truth.

Wholesome Words

That is the first distinguishing characteristic of biblical preaching that I wish to explore with you. Don't miss the fact that Christ's words are styled "wholesome" or "healthy." Healthy words produce spiritual health among members of a congregation. Certainly, the description "wholesome" refers to the content preached, but also to the very words in which that content was conveyed. How do we know that? From the context in which Paul contrasts Jesus' preaching with the insidious preaching of those who quarrel over "words." The concern, then, is to make our words worthy of the message that they proclaim.

Again, in addressing Timothy—to whom he was passing the torch in this last of his epistles—Paul reiterates, "Have the pattern of healthy words that you heard from me in the faith and love that are in Christ Jesus" (2 Timothy

1:13). Paul wanted Timothy to preserve the "good deposit" (the Gospel) that he entrusted to him unaltered (cf. v. 14). But note, in addition, that the means by which they were to be passed down was through a "pattern" of "words." A pattern of healthy words requires more than accurate content, as important as that is; it also implies that Paul formed and set forth this content in words that should be appropriated and used by Timothy. It was almost as if he has set forth a statement of faith or a creed. The words, he says, "were healthy." Paul enlarged on that point when he told Timothy that he himself would be "nourished by the words of the faith and of the good teaching" that he had "followed closely" (1 Timothy 4:6).

Once more, in the pastoral epistle to Titus, listen to Paul: "But as for you, speak things that are in keeping with healthy teaching" (Titus 2:1). Here he stresses the teaching itself. But just as in the letters to Timothy, it is also the language in which this message was taught that he is concerned about: "exhibit ... integrity in your teaching, seriousness, and healthy speech that cannot be censored" (Titus 2:7-8). If this matter is of such vital importance to Paul when addressing younger preachers, it should be to us as well.

Authoritative Words

When Jesus had finished preaching the Sermon on the Mount, we read, "Now the result was that ... the crowds were astonished at His teaching" (Matthew 7:28). What was it that amazed them? Matthew continues, "He taught them as an authority and not as their scribes" (v. 29). Of all that might have been said about that matchless message, it surely is instructive to note that it was the authority with which Jesus preached that impressed the crowds.

Their comment is that Jesus' teaching was quite unlike that which they were receiving from their scribes. Scribes originally were those who copied out and cared for the Scriptures. Because of their familiarity with the Bible, in time they became teachers of the law—preachers. But their preaching and teaching lacked authority. Jesus' words cut through traditions and man-made rules and regulations. This fact was what struck the people who heard Him. His preaching was different—it was backed by absolute authority. Scribes didn't preach that way. Instead (as anyone can readily confirm by consulting the Talmud), they spent their time "wrangling over words." Debating with one another over every jot and tittle, they brought an uncertain message to their hearers. Indeed, much of their teaching took the form, "Rabbi Shammai says ... but Rabbi Hillel says." That is an example of unhealthy teaching.

In the Middle Ages, preaching was wedded to allegory. Accordingly, almost any meaning might be squeezed out of any text. Bernard, an avowed mystic who believed in allegory and three levels of interpretation, went so far as to say to those listening to him preach, "If this interpretation does not please you, then there is another."[4] Sounds a lot like the scribes, doesn't it?

Unfortunately, there is a tendency in some Christian circles today to do much the same thing as the scribes did. Rather than set forth in clear, unequivocal words what a passage means, many writers and preachers "give an uncertain sound." I have been reading a book on preaching this past week in which the author takes the better part of a ream of paper to say what could have been said in one-fourth of the space he used. He seems quite concerned about quoting other writers, discussing their views, and filling his book with footnotes. But the average pastor, harassed as he is today, doesn't have time to wade through all of that. He needs help in preaching, and he needs it right away. Let *him* judge whether or not the writer's conclusions are correct. Forget the others whose views he spends an inordinate amount of space reviewing and evaluating. Instead of exhibiting his scholarship, the writer might have helped many more men if he had spoken more authoritatively about his views of preaching. I dare say that if they buy the book, many will miss the good things that the author has to say because they will put it down after a chapter or three. A book about preaching ought to exhibit the same healthy qualities that amazed the crowd.

The failure to state explicitly what one thinks is a problem of today's pulpit. This is manifested in several ways, a couple of which I shall mention. First, there is little direct preaching about hell and other hard doctrines. Indeed, this very author I have been reading doesn't come out and say there is a hell; he couches his words in terminology that indicates men will be "separated" from God. That is true, of course, but it is also true that the Bible speaks of the "lake of fire" and the "smoke" of "torment rising forever." The author's version is sanitized. When we tone down language, using euphemisms, for instance, we take away from the authority with which Jesus and the apostles preached.

---

4   St. Bernard, *On the Song of Songs*. A.R. Nowbray (London: 1952), p. 116.

It is, however, not only the hard doctrines that must be preached authoritatively, it is also those that state the great facts of salvation. Inferior preaching, for instance, makes people wonder whether, once saved, they may be lost again. It may leave doubt in a congregation's mind whether there will be a resurrection of the body if a preacher speaks only of the immortality of the soul. Fuzzy teaching about the second coming opens a congregation to the latest nonsense on "Christian" TV or in books sold at Walmart. And so it goes.

The second way that truth is not stated as authoritatively as it ought to be is by the weak language that is used by so many preachers. When they say, "I 'feel' that so and so is true," they detract from the authoritative message God has called them to deliver. When they speak of "sharing" they significantly diminish the message as well. Rather than expressing "feelings" or "sharing" they ought to be declaring, proclaiming, preaching, and affirming. Language makes a difference!

The fallacy that words don't matter as long as the message is preached couldn't be more ruinous. It leads to wholesome and non-authoritative preaching. To be sloppy about the choice of words is to confuse or even misdirect people. And that too is serious! We are not talking about proclaiming men's ideas, but the very Word of the living God.

I have described two forms of biblical preaching. The question now is, "What makes preaching wholesome? How does it get that way?" The two issues discussed give some initial hints, but it is now time to dig more deeply into the matter. We must know what it is that makes preaching biblical.

Chapter Two
A Case in Point

I promised to explore how you may learn to use wholesome words preached authoritatively to persuade your listeners. As we begin, let's look at a prime example of one who admirably did this. His name is John the Baptist.

Look at the Results

That he was persuasive ought to be apparent to anyone who reads the New Testament. We learn that "crowds … came out to be baptized by John" (Luke 3:7). But, in comparison with the other Gospel accounts, it is clear that Luke's report is really quite conservative. Matthew tells us that "Jerusalem, all Judea and the whole Jordan River region went out to him, and were baptized by him at the Jordan River …" (Matthew 3:5-6; cf. Mark 1:5, whose account is similar). Of course, Matthew didn't intend for anyone to take his words literally. What he meant was that there was a mass exodus out of the city of Jerusalem and from the neighboring regions into the desert to hear this man preach. When they did, it was clear that he got the results he was looking for because throngs were baptized by him.

It is instructive to note that John's preaching was not "sweet" in the modern sentimental sense of the word (see Luke 3:7–9). But as we saw in the Introduction, that word means persuasive enough to those who listen to elicit a favorable response from them. The response in this instance was confession of sin and baptism—something that isn't always easy to accomplish (as every preacher knows). It will do us well, then, to take a look at John's preaching and discover what it was in his preaching that God used to bring this about.

John's Message

John had a double message. From the prophecy of Isaiah, he proclaimed the coming of the Lord Jesus Christ. Indeed, as Isaiah said, he was sent to "prepare" His way. As the forerunner (or advance man) of Jesus, he caused quite a stir that led to the expectation that the Messiah was coming. Jesus followed in his train, and because John's ministry was highly successful, He was immediately able to draw enormous crowds of listeners as well. John's other message from Malachi was a warning of fearful judgment about to come and, in the light of that fact, the need for repentance (cf. Luke 3:8-9).[1]

Jesus' Estimate of John

Commenting upon John's outstanding ministry Jesus said "a person greater than John the Baptist hasn't arisen" (Matthew 11:11). He called John a "burning and shining lamp" and said that his followers "were willing to enjoy his light for a time" (John 5:35). These words of highest commendation from our Lord ought to make us pause to study the preaching of the Baptist. Here, without a doubt, was a man of God who knew how to preach persuasively. How did he do so?

The Gospel

Well, first, it is important to understand that he preached a pure Gospel message. Pointing to Jesus he declared, "Here is God's Lamb, Who will take away the world's sins" (John 1:29; see also v. 36). He explained that his ministry was "to reveal Him to Israel," and for that purpose he came "baptizing with water" (John 1:31). In addition, John said, "I have seen and I testify that He is God's Son" (John 1:34). And he predicted that just as he baptized with water, Jesus would baptize with the Holy Spirit (John 1:33).

John declared that Jesus is the "Light that gives light" to all who "receive Him" by faith (John 1:9-12). And he carefully distinguished between himself and the "prophet" that Moses predicted would come (John 1:21). There was nothing fuzzy about what John taught. Everything he said was etched out as sharply as it could be. Listen to him responding to the priests and Levites from Jerusalem who asked, "Who are you?" (John 1:19). We read, "He confessed (and didn't deny it) 'I am not the Christ' " (John 1:20; 3:28). Rather, he identified himself with the person in Isaiah's prophecy who would be "the voice of one shouting in the desert, 'Make the Lord's way straight' " (John 1:23). Clearly, there was nothing uncertain about what John taught. His preaching was straightforward and precise. Indeed, he showed such

---

1   The destruction of Jerusalem in 70AD.

deference to Jesus that on one occasion he said, "He must increase, but I must decrease" (John 3:30). By this he meant that his very effective work would trail off as Jesus' greater work would begin. To finally complete his task he was able to make a transition from himself to the Lord Jesus Christ.

Characteristics of John's Preaching

As we look at this highly effective ministry, we notice additional characteristics. John preached with utter clarity. He was not hesitant to proclaim eternal judgment. His entire ministry pointed to Jesus Christ. He made crucial distinctions between himself and Jesus. He preached the death of Christ, the Lamb, for sinners. And he called for faith in Him as the Messianic Son of God. That is healthy teaching. It stands in stark contrast to much of the weak, insipid, hesitant, and touchy-feely preaching that occurs today. All those who want to be persuasive need to learn these basic facts from John's preaching.

As we continue, we will consider some of these characteristics of healthy, authoritative preaching separately in detail. If there is anything in this politically correct world that could cut through the fog, it is teaching like John's. Whether they themselves know it or not, people are starved for such preaching. The bumps of sin and the ruts of iniquity in the road to redemption that John repaired by his preaching of repentance made a smooth path for the message of salvation that came through Jesus Christ. The same can be true in a lesser sense today. Those who preach as he did, by calling for repentance, level the road for the coming of Jesus into the lives of their listeners.

Chapter Three
Clarity

As we have seen, John's preaching was clear. No one need misunderstand what he had to say. If one did, it was because he did not want to understand. We have mentioned some of the characteristics of John's preaching, a number of which contributed to the clarity of his teaching.

Straightforward Preaching

Consider first the simple, straightforward language that he used. Like his Lord, what he had to say was immediately understandable. He used no academic or technical terms. He spoke in everyday speech, using single, graphic words that everyone knew. He did not hesitatingly wander about his subject; he simply came out and said what he had to say. Today, those who have been nurtured in the schools have a difficult time shaking off the language habits of academia. Many professors seem to relish jargon, complexity, and obtuseness. This is so for several reasons—not all of which pertain to any one professor. Some seem to think that if they can make a subject sound difficult the students will respect them because they sound profound. While probably only a few consciously do so, many may have fallen into patterns that they know will get a wider hearing from those who read the specialized journals to which they may contribute articles from time to time. Unless studded with footnotes, such articles are considered unscholarly. In pursuing a Ph.D., students are expected to fill their required doctoral dissertations with such references.

Avoid Verbal Footnotes and Qualifications

The supreme effort that every doctoral student makes in writing the dull, obscure dissertation sets a pattern that often carries over into subsequent writing—and even into preaching. Although there are no footnotes in preaching, something approximating them often appears: qualifications and quotations. Both of these ought to be used with great caution and only infrequently. They detract from the force of what is said and lessen the speaker's authority. You simply cannot find John qualifying his remarks. Words like "perhaps," "possibly," and "some think, but others aver …" are conspicuously absent. He did quote from Isaiah and Malachi, but not to set forth the range of varying viewpoints from which to choose as some modern preachers do. Unlike the scribes, he quoted the prophets as absolute authorities whose predictions he was fulfilling. As a result, he left no doubts about the fact that both his message and his work were God-ordained.

Scripture, Not Speculation

It would be better for a preacher not to speak at all than to offer his congregation speculations, uncertainties, or even possibilities. A preacher, like John, is a herald of the King sent to declare His Word. While he is not an inspired apostle or even a prophet like John, his task is still to proclaim a message from the inspired inscripturated Word of God. From his heart he should be able to say, "Thus saith the Lord." To qualify his statements so that the clarity of the message is mitigated is to fail in his calling.

There is no need to speculate. In the Scriptures we have everything we need for life (salvation) and godliness (sanctification; see 2 Peter 1:3; 2 Timothy 3:15; John 17:17). What is to be ours is "revealed;" what is not belongs to God (Deuteronomy 29:29). Moreover, the Scriptures are no allegory behind which one must discover some hidden or mystic meaning: "Therefore, whatever lies plain on the surface of God's Word, not in one phrase alone, but in many places, that is exceedingly apt to be what is meant."[1] Further explaining his words, this same author says, "… we shall be most likely to get its meaning more clearly and truly if we take the plain meaning of the passage that lies on the surface to any sophisticated observer."[2]

Clear Understandings

How does a preacher learn to be clear? Well, first, he must have a clear understanding of his preaching portion and what he will say about it. That means he must engage in the careful, long, and hard work of exegesis. That is necessary for him to say with dead certainty, "This is what God teaches us

---

[1] John Broadus, *Favorite Sermons of John Broadus*. Harper (NY: 1959), p. 55.
[2] Ibid.

in the passage before us this morning." Careless work in the study accounts for much of the non-persuasive preaching that takes place. If he doesn't have a clear understanding himself, how can he hope to make the message clear to his hearers?

Matching Language to Truth

Next, his language choices—and they are that—ought to match the truth he preaches as closely as possible. They should not be "nearly right" words and phrases, but those that fit exactly. And this fit must include connotative mood as well as factual denotation. For instance, he ought to use robust language, as John did, when he pronounced judgment upon the religious leaders of his generation (see Luke 3:7-9). His figures of speech vividly pictured the utter destruction to come as well. Cutting trees down with an axe (Luke 3:9) and shoveling chaff into the fire (Matthew 3:12) graphically portrayed the impending holocaust. Nothing less than such language choices would have been satisfactory. Lesser figures of speech and tamer language would have persuaded far fewer people.

Trim Off the Fat

Clarity was also achieved by eliminating unnecessary words. Wordiness is difficult to follow, and listeners tend to lose the thread of what is being said. On the other hand, shorter, exact terminology and phraseology tend to be clear. Sometimes, it is well to couch a message in a brief, memorable form as John's words did when he said, "He must increase, but I must decrease" (John 3:30). Here is a more recent one: "The devil may tempt a hardworking Christian, but an idle Christian tempts the devil."[3] Brief, direct, punctuated language gets results.

Making the Complex Simple

If he takes the time to think about how to do so, a preacher can make any truth clear—no matter how difficult or complex it may be. But it will take work. He must be absolutely certain about the truth himself, as I said above, and then he must work on how to bring that home to his congregation. Good preaching is not merely a matter of good exegesis, as some

---

3   Alexander McLaren, *A Rosary of Christian Graces*. Horace Marshall & Son. (London: 1899), p. 122, 123.

seem to think; it is also a matter of careful thought about how to say what must be said. All too few take the necessary care to word truth properly to achieve this end. Consequently, by hurrying the sermon along, they muddy an already difficult teaching so that it becomes nearly unintelligible.

Preachers ought to take the Lord's preaching as the supreme example of simple (not simplistic) preaching. Eldersveld said, "He made everything so simple, so easy to understand."[4]

Eliminate Vagueness

Clarity and vague terminology always clash. To use words like "things" rather than to enumerate them by name obscures. There was nothing indefinite about John's preaching. Each word was chosen so as not to confuse or mislead. When asked for direction about how to grow the fruit of repentance he told people exactly what to do (Luke 3:10-14). He gave explicit, concrete answers rather than leaving them with abstract generalizations. He didn't say, "Well, go back to your homes and find some way to help the poor." No, he said, "Give them your extra shirt!" He didn't even tell the soldiers to stop complaining; he said, "Quit this grousing about your paycheck!" That is preaching with clarity.

There is a classic spoof on this problem that most recently appeared in the *Woodruff* (SC) *News*, September 11, 2003, a portion of which follows.

… after every flight, pilots fill out a form called a gripe sheet, which conveys to the mechanics problems encountered with the aircraft … the latter read and correct the problems, and then respond … on the lower half of the form what remedial action was taken … Here are some actual logged … complaints by Qantas pilots and the solutions recorded …

- Problem: Left inside main tire almost needs replacement.
  Solution: Almost replaced left inside main tire.
- Problem: Something loose in cockpit.
  Solution: Something tightened in cockpit.
- Problem: Evidence of leaks on right main landing gear.
  Solution: Evidence removed.
- Problem: DME volume unbelievably loud.
  Solution: DME volume set to more believable level.

---

4   Peter Eldersveld, *Nothing but the Gospel.* Eerdmans (Grand Rapids: 1966), p. 157.

- Problem: Suspected crack in windshield.
  Solution: Suspect you are right.

I will not comment on this list of problems and "solutions." If you don't get the point, then comment would be useless! Rather, let me direct you to the words of a wise preacher who recognized the importance of specificity. He introduces a message on John 3:18 this way:

> The idea of sin in general is vague and unimpressive. Any particular sin would hardly be applicable to all, and some who are not wholly innocent will excuse themselves by thinking others much more guilty. But the text presents a sin of which all who hear it are guilty, all without exception, all alike—the sin of unbelief.[5]

Use Everyday Speech

Clarity is also achieved by speaking in the listener's everyday language. There wasn't a single word John uttered that his listeners couldn't understand *on the spot*. Preachers who use bookish terms fail to realize that spoken language greatly differs from written language. For instance, the reader may read at his leisure and at his own pace. The listener must get the message right then and there at the speaker's rate of delivery. The reader may pull down a dictionary and look up words he doesn't quite understand; the listener cannot do so. He must understand every term as it is spoken. Nevertheless, John was careful not to speak down to his audience, but he did speak plainly on their level.

The problem of purple prose and oratory is no longer the threat that it once was to persuasive preaching. But there are preachers who still attempt to be ornate. Jefferson has a word for those who may be tempted to drift into it: "Sermons ... are primary forms of food [for sheep].... If this could be remembered it would help many a minister to get rid of his stilted English ... rhetorical ruffles ... bombastic elocution and skyrocketing perorations."[6]

Make Careful Distinctions

John was deeply concerned about truth. He would not, for instance, allow his listeners to confuse him with the Messiah. So, he explicitly said

---
5   John Broadus, *Favorite Sermons of John Broadus*. Harper (NY: 1959), p. 136.
6   Charles Edward Jefferson, *The Ministering Shepherd* (YMCA: Paris), p. 61.

that he was not the Christ. He must have recognized that clarity is a close cousin of truth while obscurity is akin to error.

Thomas Guthrie provides an excellent example of drawing distinctions in his book, *The Gospel in Ezekiel*: "… we must be careful not to confound pity with mercy… Mercy is a higher attribute … we pity simple suffering; but let pity and love be extended to *guilty* suffering and you have the very element of mercy." Again, in distinguishing inner from outer change he says, "… the change is on the man within … on the tenant, not the tenement." And "We are all saved by grace, but shall be tried by works." And, of course, he goes on to explain these statements further, even illustrating the differences involved.[7]

Use Appropriate Language

To be persuasive, a preacher's words must be appropriate to the thoughts he wants to convey or they will mislead. Return for a minute to John's description of the judgment to come. He didn't use an illustration having to do with ice or cold. Rather, he spoke of shoveling people into unquenchable fire. Fire is a far more appropriate term for judgment than ice or snow.

Be Light on Adjectives

Note that John used very few adjectives when preaching, but whenever he did, they carried considerable weight. The "fire" he noted would be "unquenchable." That is an important fact—it will be unending and without relief. Nor does John say such things as "Hell will be horrible." Instead, he describes it so that the truth that it is horrible is the thought that arises in the heart of his listeners. When a preacher has to tell people how to react to what he is saying, he is not preaching clearly enough to engage the listener's thoughts and emotions. It's almost as bad as having to explain a joke.

Brevity is Important

And John was brief. Complex sentences and rambling darken truth by making the preacher's words difficult to follow. He must get right to the point. Otherwise, people will be saying (or at least thinking), "What's he

---

7   Thomas Guthrie, *The Gospel in Ezekiel*. Zondervan (Grand Rapids: n.d.), pp. 159, 160, 251, 332.

getting at?" Their grammar may not be the best, but their objection to fuzzy speech is right on target.

End Confusion

As I have already noted, John was careful to make clear distinctions. He meticulously distinguished himself from the "Light" as well as from the "Prophet" and the "Christ," about which the people questioned him. He was only the "voice," as he said. It was unmistakable where he stood in reference to Jesus—he was unworthy to untie his sandals! He would not allow people to become confused about the matter. (See John 1). Unlike the way John left his audience, preachers today often leave theirs confused. Congregations need clear instruction in order to help them see things more sharply. They usually appreciate it when a preacher discriminates between things that differ. And when he is able to help them sort things out this way, he is usually persuasive.

Fearless Preaching Required

Finally, clarity comes from fearless preaching. John denounced Herod for his sin in no uncertain terms, knowing how dangerous it was to do so. Herod, and those around him, certainly got the point! Even though he was put to death for it, John believed it was his duty before God to do it. Today, preachers are afraid to preach biblical truth clearly because someone might be offended and leave the church. Clear preaching is often avoided by those who speak with temporal consequences in mind. The word translated "bold" throughout the book of Acts, used to describe the apostles' preaching, is *parresia*. It means "speaking clearly without fear of consequences." There is a need for such fearless preaching in today's church! Perhaps preachers who have this problem ought to pray the "Preacher's Prayer" found in Acts 4:29.

So now, Lord, take note of their threats and give Your slaves all the boldness needed to speak Your word.

Chapter Four

Confrontation

Biblical preaching, like biblical counseling, is always confrontational. That observation raises the hackles of many, I realize. They think of confrontation as harsh and unloving. When I described Nouthetic Counseling as "Nouthetic Confrontation" I got all sorts of negative reactions from those who misunderstood (as well as from those who wanted to!). So, at the outset let me explain what I mean by "confrontation."

Not What You've Heard

Confrontation may be harsh and judgmental when it ought not to be, but saying that it is essential to the meaning of the word is wrong. By confrontation, I mean dealing with problems rather than evading them.[1] I mean also that people are confronted with God's Word in such a way that they may not misunderstand or avoid it. The term does not necessarily involve confronting in order to judge or condemn. A person may be confronted directly with the great truths of the Gospel of Grace in order to persuade him to trust Christ and be saved. That is what John the Baptist did. Without a doubt, he was a confrontational preacher. Do you think that John's heart was cold and hard when he preached repentance? His ministry was designed to "turn the hearts of the fathers to their children and to turn the hearts of the children to their fathers" (Malachi 4:6). Could a man whose own heart was not so "turned" persuasively carry out such a mission in the way that John did?

Blessings in Confrontation

A Christian may be confronted with the facts of assurance and eternal life and other uplifting and comforting truths in order to encourage and build

---

[1] Just exactly as here I am dealing with the problem posed by the word "confrontation."

him up in his faith. This ministry of positive preaching is confrontational in that it makes sure that no one misses out on God's blessings. Ordinarily it will be carried out with great joy and expectation. It is like confronting the winner of the Reader's Digest prize. You know what happens—the award is taken to the winner's doorstep and presented to him directly. The intention (besides the publicity angle involved) is to be sure that it is delivered to him personally. "Confrontation," then, carries the connotation that persuasion is personal. Such preaching helps the listener know that what is being said pertains to him personally. It was said of Mark Twain that when he lectured, "he had a button-hole relationship with his audience."[2] Should anything less be said of God's herald?

Direct Preaching

So, by "confrontation" I mean speaking directly to people about truth—whether or not it may be bringing some good news or calling for repentance (and, of course, the two should always be connected). The word is a large one, but one that ought not to be avoided because it best describes what is necessary to truly persuasive preaching.

Here is a sample of Spurgeon's preaching that shows how the direct preaching of good news can encourage a believer: "Dear brethren, what a day it will be for the righteous! For some of them were—perhaps some here present are—lying under some very terrible accusation of which they are perfectly guiltless."[3]

Crowds

Let's think about confrontation and persuasion for a bit. We would like to move crowds as John did, to be sure. But so often the crowds are fickle, as we see in the case of those who followed Jesus. One day they cried "Hosanna!" and the next "Crucify him!" That is the trouble with crowds. When crowds are truly persuaded to believe or do God's will, that is because the members in the crowd are individually persuaded and not just influenced as a part of some emotionally charged situation. The "persuasion" of the latter sort of crowds will stick. The enthusiasm, which is like that of those Jesus called rocky soil on which the seed of the Word was sown, but can't

---

2   Justin Caplan, *Mr. Clemens and Mark Twain*. Simon and Shuster (NY: 1966), p. 34.
3   C.H. Spurgeon, *The Great Assize*. Scripture Truth Depot, p. 6.

last since there is no depth in them, describes crowds that are moved by crowd-generated emotionalism rather than truth. That is not the "persuasion" that ought to be sought. Yet, the preachers of large congregations often gather people of that sort. One reason for this is that they fail to confront them with the claims of God's truth. Their services and their sermons are calculated to bring in numbers. It is not that numbers cannot be persuaded as they ought to be—John proved that to be false. But for crowds to respond, as they ought—in ways that are lasting and produce fruit—they will always respond to preaching that confronts them personally.

Personal Preaching

What does "personal" preaching mean, and what does it look like? When confrontational preaching is successful in God's eyes, it is preaching that is personal in that individuals understand that the preacher's message is actually a message from God. They are confronted with God Himself as a result of what is preached. As the Scriptures are "opened," their hearts "burn[ed] within" them (Luke 24:32). And their eyes are opened to behold wonderful things out of God's law.

How does this happen? What must a preacher do to make sure that individuals consider themselves confronted by God as they are confronted with His Word? For one thing, preachers must preach as heralds. The herald has nothing of his own to offer; he is merely a messenger of his king. Preachers who call attention to themselves, their interests, their concerns, and their ideas distract from godly confrontation. Sadly, this is often the norm rather than the exception. How many preachers use the first person plural and singular as the dominant mode in which their sermons are cast? The words "we" and "I" occur over and over again. Most of their illustrations even come from events that happened to them. Such matters, you may be sure, detract from the King and His Word.

Two Key Words

But how should confrontational preaching take place then? Two words ought to dominate preaching: "God" and "you." The preacher must make sure that his congregation understands that he is bringing a message from God to each one of them. And therefore, most frequently, his use of the second person should be the use of the second person *singular* ("you" as an individual). How he preaches will make that clear. He will often say such things as, "*God calls each one of you* to do this" and "Now, don't think of the person sitting next to you when you hear what God has to say in this passage. This is God's message to *you*." In other words, he will preach confrontationally. He will preach the Bible as a contemporary Book. What does that mean? Well, in the next chapter we shall see.

Chapter Five
Contemporaneity

Christian sermons are preached from material that is several thousand years old, composed in distant lands, and written in foreign languages. How then can preaching be contemporary?

The Bible itself tells us that it is to be considered a contemporary book.

> *Now these events happened to them as examples and were recorded as counsel for us who live at this late date in history (1 Corinthians 10:11).*

> *Whatever was written before was written for our instruction (Romans 15:4).*

Paul's Stance Toward Scripture

There can be no doubt, then, that the apostle Paul considered Scripture to be addressed not only to those for whom it was originally written, but also for those living in later times. Moreover, the Bible was not only for Jews, but for Gentiles as well. Since he was writing to those who spoke Greek, and not Hebrew or Aramaic, Paul expected Christians who read some early form of the Septuagint[1] to proclaim God's truth from it to their contemporaries just as he did. This translation was in the contemporary language of the Mediterranean world. There has been good reason for doing so in every generation since.

Yet, one of the principal failures of preaching has been to preach sermons as if the message had to be adapted to our times in such radical ways that it seemed almost unintelligible. Typically, ministers have preached biblical truth as if it were obsolete. They seem to be talking about what happened long ago and far away at the time when God "used to do things." And they preach from the land of Palestine rather than from their own country.

---

1   The majority of Paul's quotations come from the LXX.

Indeed, all that some do is conduct sermonic "Holy Land Tours." One can hardly expect such preaching to be persuasive. It rarely touches lives at the vital spots. Paul didn't treat the Old Testament that way. He considered its message to be up to date—a message to be preached to his contemporaries because it was intended for them. If they wish to be persuasive, preachers today must adopt the same stance.

John Calvin's Preaching

One of the few preachers who captured this important truth about preaching and clearly preached Scripture as written for his congregation was John Calvin. Let me refer to just a few passages from many in his writings and sermons in which he treats the Bible as God's Word to the flock in Geneva. At the outset of a series of sermons on the book of Ephesians, Calvin's very first words are:

> When we read the epistles which St. Paul wrote to a variety of places, we must always consider that God meant that they should serve not only for one time alone, or for one people only, but forever, and in general for the whole church. And truly, if a man considers the doctrine that is contained in them well, it will be easy to discern that God's intention was to be heard in the things that are spoken there, even to the world's end.[2]

In that paragraph, Calvin set forth a philosophy of preaching that went a long way toward persuading people in Switzerland (and throughout many other places in the world) to adopt the views of the Reformation.

How does this contemporary stance toward a preaching portion work out in actual practice? Here are some typical examples of how Calvin followed his own dictum:

> And so the Holy Spirit exhorts us at this day by the same doctrine to consider our own misery that we may be humbled in ourselves and receive the inestimable benefit offered us by the gospel by the person of Christ.[3]

Here is another:

> ... all the more then we must heed Micah's admonition in this text. For it was not his intent to address the Jews only, but also to address us.[4]

---

2   John Calvin, *Sermons on the Epistle to the Ephesians.* The Banner of Truth Trust: Carlisle (1979), p. 7.
3   Ibid. p. 186.
4   Micah, op. cit., p. 137.

Similar comments are sprinkled throughout his sermons. And it is not only when he thinks to express the fact that the Scriptures have a contemporary message for us that he uses them in a contemporary way. As a rule, he simply treats his preaching portion as a message to them from God. In short, Calvin preached Scripture passages as if he had just opened up a recent letter from God addressed to his people and was exhorting them from it. This contemporary use of the Bible in preaching is persuasive. The fact is, however, whether it was persuasive or not, preachers ought to use it this way—simply because it is right to do so.

John Chrysostom

Many of the great preachers in the history of preaching recognized the need for contemporaneity. John "the golden-mouthed one" (as the name Chrysostom means) did. In his eighth homily he says, "… come now, let us see in regard to this spiritual nourishment what it is today also that the blessed Moses is teaching us through the text we've read, or rather what the grace of the Spirit has to say to us all through his tongue."[5] And in the tenth homily we read, "You see, speaking through the Spirit, this blessed author wants at this point to teach us something kept from human hearing."[6] And, he reminds his congregation, "You see, since the blessed Moses taught us yesterday how the Creator of all beautified the shapelessness of the earth …"[7]

Use Contemporary Language

Contemporary preaching ought to be done in contemporary language. Old "preacher's terms," largely growing out of King James language, are still heard from many pulpits today. I am not thinking here only about the "thee's" and the "thou's" that some use in prayer, and that still appear in sermons where preachers read the so-called Authorized Version of the Bible. No. Rather, I am thinking of the preacher's language that he uses to address his congregation. Words like "sepulchre" instead of "tomb" and "beloved" instead of "friends" are typical. Phrases like "the love of God" instead of "God's love" also exhibit this trend. The use of "for" instead of "since" or "because" is especially troublesome.

---

5 St. John Chrysostom, *Homilies on Genesis*. Robert C. Hill, trans. The Catholic University of America Press. (Washington: 1985), p. 106.
6 Ibid., p. 132.
7 Ibid., p. 82

If you want a model of how to use contemporary language, look at the sermons of Charles Swindoll. Not only is his terminology up to date, but it is even on the cutting edge of contemporary language.

Why is contemporary language more persuasive? Principally because it doesn't get in the way of understanding. When a preacher uses archaic terms or phraseology, the congregation must make the adjustment from that language to what it means in his. In doing so, he may miss the next point. In other words, archaic language makes it hard to follow the preacher's train of thought. Why create difficulties unnecessarily? In addition to this, such language calls attention to itself rather than to the thought the preacher wishes to convey. It therefore distracts. Since it is archaic, it tends to undo the contemporary relevance of the sermon. It adds to the faulty perception that the message is for a different time, place, and people. For these and other reasons, it should be clear that, in order to persuade, one must avoid all of those preaching practices that tend to weaken the impact of God's truth.

Not Slang

It is not necessary to use slang in preaching. This also has the disadvantage of calling attention to itself—and to the preacher who uses it. Members of the congregation wonder whether it is appropriate to the subject and whether or not their preacher has good judgment. In addition to that, the life of many slang words is temporary, and before he knows it, the preacher, who probably cannot keep up with changes all that closely, may be using slang that young people in the audience may consider already obsolete. Thus, the attempt to be current may backfire. His attempt to be "with it" (and this slang phrase itself seems to be almost outmoded) becomes laughable.

Language People Speak

Contemporary preaching helps persuade simply because it is the language of people *today*. That puts it simply and may say it all. Make a careful assessment of your preaching. Do you use the Bible in a contemporary way? And is the language you use also contemporary? Taking care about this manner can make a great difference.

Chapter Six
Conviction

WHEN Paul wrote "I solemnly call on you to preach the Word, be at it in season and out of season. Convict, reprove, urge with complete patience and full teaching" (2 Timothy 4:1-2), he was speaking about an aspect of persuasive preaching that is necessary, but often wanting in the modern evangelical churches.

What Conviction Is

Protruding from the list of imperatives in verse two is the word "convict." This is a legal term frequently occurring in the New Testament. For instance, in 2 Timothy 3:16, the Scriptures are said to be "useful for teaching, for conviction, for correction and for disciplined training in righteousness." And in John 16:8 we read that when the Holy Spirit comes, "He will convict the world about sin, about righteousness and about judgment." The term means to so prosecute a case against someone that he is *convicted* of the crime of which he was accused. Unlike the modern religious use of the word convict, it does not speak of a subjective feeling that one may have upon realizing he is guilty of sin. That may or may not occur. Rather, it is an objective, judicial word that indicates that a person is declared guilty—whether he accepts the verdict or not, and whether there is or isn't any particular positive, subjective response to the judgment.

What Brings It About?

What is so interesting about these three passages is that there are three distinct agents mentioned in the process of convicting people of sin. One is the preacher who, like Timothy, is ordered to convict his listeners. The second is the Scriptures, which are also said to convict. And third, the Holy Spirit is described as the One Who convicts. Reading these three statements, one might wonder whether the Bible contradicts itself. Who—or what—is it that convicts? There is no contradiction. All three, working together, bring about the verdict. The Scriptures, proclaimed by the preacher, are used by the Holy Spirit to make the case. All three, then, have a part in bringing about the conviction of a sinner. That means that preachers must preach for conviction by making a scriptural case against the guilty one, asking the Spirit to use His Word to make the biblical judgment clear to those involved.

The Preacher's Part

There are those who think that it is not the task of ministers to preach so as to "convict." Their view is that the Spirit Himself will do all of the convicting that is necessary. Of course Paul's words undercut this flawed notion. These same people, who constitute a growing group, object to the use of application. They preach little that is calculated to bring the Bible to bear upon individuals; rather, they preach the "big picture." These extreme "Biblical Theology" buffs are decidedly wrong.[1] Not only do we have Paul's command here, but we see that at the coming of the Lord Jesus Christ, when He executes judgment, He will "convict all the ungodly of all their ungodly works that they have done in an ungodly way" (Jude 15). Surely this is a judicial act in which Jesus will make the case for judging ungodly persons according to their ungodly lives. As a result, they will be consigned to eternal punishment. They will not be convicted (in the modern, subjective sense) so as to recognize their sin and repent.

So, the task of the preacher is to so marshal Scripture that he is able to make a case against those who have sinned—whether they are the unsaved mentioned in Jude, or whether they are the members of the congregation mentioned in II Timothy. He must know the Scriptures thoroughly enough to do so, and must know how to reason from the Scriptures to be able to pull it off.

Obviously, persuasion is involved in the work of the prosecutor who brings a case against an offender. And reasoning is essential in the process of doing so. But, again, there are those who say, "Never try to reason with

---

[1] Not all biblical theologians hold to these views. There is a vital place for biblical theology, but it is wrong to make preaching a biblical theological enterprise. Biblical theology is for the minister's study, where he uses it along with systematic theology to help understand the place of his passage in the history of redemption. But to speak of "Biblical Theological preaching" indicates an overemphasis upon discipline to the detriment of others.

people; simply tell them what the Bible has to say and let the Spirit do the rest." That, however, isn't what the apostles did. In Acts 17:17 we read that Paul "reasoned in the synagogue with the Jews and the God-fearing Greeks, and every day in the marketplace with those who happened to be there." And this was no isolated case. We read that "every Sabbath" at Corinth, Paul "reasoned with both the Jews and the Greeks" (Acts 18:4), and that later he "reasoned daily at Tyrannus' school" (Acts 19:9). Plainly, this was a frequent activity of the apostle who seems to have reasoned in both informal and formal settings. In order for someone to change, he must first be brought to a recognition that something needs changing. Conviction is what makes that possible.

Reasoning from the Scriptures

An insight into what Paul's reasoning was like may be found in Romans 1 through 3, where he makes the case that all Gentiles and Jews alike have sinned and need a Savior Who can justify them before God. He then goes on in the following chapters of the book to show that Jesus is that Savior, and that we may be justified only by faith in Him and His atoning work.

How was this persuasive reasoning done? Clearly, by the use of the Scriptures from which Paul and others reasoned that Jesus was the Messiah (cf. Acts 9:22; 17:2-3; 18:28). Not only was this reasoning from the Scriptures a regular activity, it seems to have been largely the method by which the Gospel was presented. For examples of what reasoning from the Scriptures was like, study the sermons and speeches in that missionary book. It was this kind of witnessing and preaching that achieved the great successes that we read about in Acts. Today, Preachers in evangelistic contexts, as well as in exhortation of believers, ought to recognize that their task is to so bring Scripture to bear upon their listeners that they are convicted of unbelief and other sins.

Calvin Again

Since I have already had occasion to refer to John Calvin's philosophy of contemporary preaching, it might be of interest to see how he blended this with preaching for conviction. In his exposition of 2 Timothy 4 he wrote, "… for it is not enough to teach, if you do not urge…. For the doctrine of [teaching about] the gospel is helped by exhortations, so as not to be without effect ... it is the part of an ambassador to enforce by arguments."[2] Note the instructive combination of words used: urge, exhort, effect, enforce, argument. Plainly, Calvin is in line with Paul. The effect he sought was conviction as a means of persuading.

He continues: "Ministers are here taught that it is not enough simply to advance doctrine. They must also labor that it may be received by the hearers ... They must not only offer ... the grace of God, but strive with all their might, that it may not be offered in vain"[3] And as a caution, in order not to stress emotion over thought, he adds: "An exhortation does not exclude doctrine ... it is properly the office of the teacher to utter no new thing of his own brain, but to apply the Scriptures."[4]

So, as an important addition to the elements involved in preaching that persuades, conviction must be included as one component. I cannot urge strongly enough that people must be brought to recognize their sins through conviction,[5] which is brought about by the Holy Spirit using the Scriptures ministered in a reasoned fashion. Without these factors, persuasion will fail.

---

2 *Calvin's Commentaries, Vol. 20*, p. 244.
3 Ibid.
4 Ibid. Vol. 18, p. 514.
5 Or brought to the conviction of the truth of some biblical teaching.

Chapter Seven

Concern

Emotion Isn't Enough

Some might speak of the motivating factor that I am about to discuss as "emotion." For a time, along with others, I used to speak of adding an "emotional appeal" to the logical, exegetical presentation of biblical truth. But since then I have revised that way of thinking. While emotion is certainly involved in persuasive preaching, it isn't correct to claim that it is an adequate adjunct to reasoning that will truly persuade anyone of God's truth. Even when it is but a part of the entire presentation that is so. Emotion too often leads to superficial acceptance (infatuation?) of truth that doesn't last. People may be persuaded to follow crowds or adopt teaching that appeals to their emotions, but *concern* is a greater force for good than emotion.

It is out of concern for their eternal safety that the crowds came to John. That was what he had in mind when he cried out, "Who warned you to flee from the coming wrath?" (Luke 3:7). Here, the emotion we call fear surely was involved. But that wasn't all. Though sinners, those who came were sincerely motivated by something more than the emotion of fear. From John's preaching they learned about the wrath to come, it is true. But the Spirit had regenerated them so as to understand the facts of salvation that he presented. The truth John preached about Jesus as the Son of God caused great concern. The people learned that they had been estranged from the living God and that, finally, after four hundred years of silence, God was visiting His people again. Those who were genuinely moved to faith and action recognized that they must be baptized and trust in the Messiah, God's Lamb, as John taught.

People are not merely moved by fear; they are also moved by joy, greed, and the whole gamut of emotions. But concern for oneself, for a child, for a person in danger, for the salvation of a loved one runs deeper than mere emotion. Concern is greater and more lasting than emotion. One is not so easily turned aside from a genuine concern by other passing interests as he might be when motivated by emotion. Concern abides, and when emotion has subsided, it gnaws away at a person until something is done to satisfy it. That is why in dealing with the element in persuasion usually called emotion, I shall refer to it—and more—as concern.

Caused by Biblical Preaching

Biblical preaching causes concern in listeners. There is nothing in Scripture that should not concern us. But at times, one fact seems of more concern to a congregation than others because of its immediate relevance to them. Relevance is a principal factor in arousing concern. But often, if a matter isn't in the immediate purview of the members of a congregation, it may be brought to their attention by the right sort of introduction to the sermon. Good preaching creates concern by how a subject is introduced. Illustrations that pertain to the lives of listeners are of particular value. Without seeing what the message will mean to them, many members take a "So what?" attitude. Pastors, therefore, must give sufficient attention to how they bring a matter before their congregations. If concern is not generated early in the sermon, it will be difficult to generate it at some later point. By then many may have mentally turned off and tuned out. When concern is aroused early in a message (the earlier the better is the rule), members will consider *all* that follows important.

The concern that a preacher brings to his congregation may be concern about oneself, about others, or about the honor of God. Good preaching brings up such matters in powerful ways. Even when either of the first two concerns just mentioned looms large, the final one—God's honor—must be the backdrop for it, or it will be an unbiblical concern. The Bible is a book filled with matters that ought to concern us; on every page, rightly understood, there is something that should be a matter of concern. For instance, Peter writes, "If you call Him Father ... then be deeply concerned about how you behave during your residence as aliens" (1 Peter 1:17). Notice it is God's Fatherhood that is at stake in the behavior of His children. People say, "Like son, like Father!" In one way or another, true concern always involves pleasing God.

But because such matters may not protrude so clearly, a preacher may have to stir up concern about them. He may say, "Here is an issue that should cause concern on your part: 'May Your will be done on earth as it is in heaven' (Matthew 6:10). At first that prayer may not occasion much concern. But if you pray this with understanding, you will be concerned about what you are asking for." The preacher must then help them recognize what is at stake. When he is able to do so, he will rightly become concerned about the answer to that prayer. Indeed, good preachers show how this prayer should arouse concern for the radical transformation of his home, his community, and his church that will drive him to do what he can to see that God's will is done in these spheres. Thus, the Scriptures, opened for the members of a congregation by a faithful preacher, bring about proper concerns in the hearts of God's people. As a result, they pray about and work for change as they have not before.

John's Preaching Caused Concern

What do you think it was that led multitudes to come to John the Baptist with questions like "What then should we do?" (Luke 3:10)? Clearly, there was concern. They were not satisfied with their repentance until they knew specifically what it would entail in their everyday lives. That was real concern! We read that "the people were in a state of expectation and everybody was wondering in his heart about John, whether he might be the Christ" (Luke 3:15). It was his preaching that caused this concern. John's kind of preaching stirred people enough to raise concerns in their hearts that drove them to serious thought and action. Every preacher has been given this task. A preacher who seeks to persuade, therefore, would be wise to study John's preaching so that he may learn to do likewise. Moreover, once John got the ball rolling, he did not let up, but pushed harder: "So with many other words John encouraged [or "persuaded;" the term *parakaleo* can have either meaning] and announced the good news to the people" (Luke 3:18).

Consider Paul, Too

Listen to what drove Paul through trials and persecution of every sort: In 2 Corinthians 5:11 he expressed a concern that was nearly the top priority for his ministry: "knowing about the fear of the Lord, we persuade people." Above all else, however, his first concern was to please God: "we make it our ambition to please Him" (2 Corinthians 5:9). Great as his love for people was, to bring salvation to them was, nonetheless, only second. He knew that pleasing God must always come first. In arousing concern among his people, a preacher must always keep that primary goal in mind. They too must learn to put first things first. Unlike those who merely stir people emotionally, faithful preachers are concerned above all else to help others become concerned about glorifying God. This will usually cause their listeners to set goals in a proper order of priority, leading to courses of action designed to achieve those goals. And then, like Paul, they also will stick to them through thick and thin.

But Emotion Has Its Place

Although emotion alone is insufficient, you must never ignore it. Preaching is not delivering polite essays. People must be stirred. Calvin said, "It is lively preaching of the gospel, when persons are not merely told what is right, but are pricked (Acts 2:37)" that is necessary to good preaching.[1] Later in the same book he declared, "… the use of God's word is not only to teach … but to rouse us to a serious meditation of those things which we already understand, and not to suffer us to grow torpid in a cold knowledge."[2]

Preachers Without Concern

When a preacher has lost his concern, he will persuade no one. When a man enters the pulpit he should be fired with a desire to see change in those who hear what he has to say. This desire ought to arise out of a concern to exalt God and His Word—a concern that expresses itself in a strong desire for the salvation and the sanctification of his listeners. To this end, he will prepare his messages thoughtfully and carefully. Because of his concern, he will never neglect his preaching. For a person to enter the pulpit blandly, without a burning desire to help his people, is for him to repudiate his calling and dishonor the One Who called him.

Ministers who are simply hanging on till retirement, who have long since lost their sense of true ministry, will rarely (if ever) bring about concern for the things of God among the members of their congregations.[3] Their

---

1 *Commentaries, Vol. 22*, p. 104.
2 Ibid., p. 434.
3 Of course, if He wills, God can bring about great things as the result of a preacher's feeble efforts. But that doesn't let him off the hook. He is responsible to prepare in con-

lackluster, routine manner of preaching, however, may cause concern about whether or not he ought to be retained by the congregation. At least it ought to. There are too many men in the ministry marking time who don't know where else to go or what else to do. They have lost any concern that they once had, and as a result certainly can't impart concern to others. Their overwhelming concern is for themselves. To bring about proper concern in others, ordinarily the preacher himself must first be concerned about God and others.

Until such preachers once more manifest this proper sense of their calling, they should take a sabbatical. If, after a time of contemplation, prayer, and confession of sin, their concern for biblical ministry does not return, they should consider going for counseling. There is something radically wrong with a preacher who has lost his concern for God's glory and the welfare of his people. That fact itself should greatly concern all who are concerned! Perhaps a Nouthetic Counselor would be able to help him refurbish his former love. At any rate, if his conscience isn't seared, there ought to be one thing that concerns him greatly—his lack of concern!

What Concern Does for a Preacher

Concern may manifest itself in a preacher going to great lengths to honor God and bless His people. In lieu of those things mentioned in the long lists of hardships that were endured by the apostle Paul (found in 2 Corinthians 6 and 11), modern preachers ought to be willing to staunchly stand up to the many adverse winds of our time that rage against the church. This may mean exposing themselves to criticism, ostracism, or even persecution of various sorts (in this country, at this juncture in time, it may be relatively mild).

In time, the concerned preacher will produce a congregation full of concerned people. That, of course, is what he is there to do. His congregation will be eager to hear what God has to say through him each Sunday. They will study Scripture during the week. And, when they encounter problems they cannot solve, they will seek help. And as Peter said, they will be deeply concerned about their behavior. They are, as he noted, aliens in this world. They are citizens of heaven. As such, they live in a hostile environment

---

cern. And when God does bless in spite of him, it should stir him to renew the concern that was previously lacking.

where the populace is watching, waiting to catch them in faults. When this happens, they use these as an excuse for not coming to Christ ("Agh ... Christians are only a gang of hypocrites"). Concern about this result will cause them to care about how their behavior affects the honor of their Lord. Lest there be any offence, the apostle John made it clear that the missionaries he sent were to take no support from the world "because they went out on behalf of the Name, taking nothing from the Gentiles" (3 John 7).

The Preacher as Model

All in all, probably there is nothing more important for a preacher to possess than a keen concern for those things we have been enumerating. He will not preach persuasively until out of his own concern, he creates concern in his listeners. His concern will become evident and will be catching. Because people do imitate, he must sincerely wish to be one who may safely be imitated by other Christians. Paul wrote to Timothy that he was to "become a model for believers in speech, in behavior, in faithfulness and in purity" (1 Timothy 4:12). Can it be said of you that your concern provides a good model for others? If there is something lacking—and in which of us aren't there many things?—then the remedy is to continue reading in 1 Timothy 5:13-16 and practice what you read.

Chapter Eight
Concreteness

Much of our language originated in pictures. Sometimes these go so far back that we have difficulty tracing them into the present. Other pictures are right up front. Numerous words have a Greek or Latin origin, so that unless one has a knowledge of these languages and can trace the English back to one of them, the picture will elude him.[1] Looking around my study as I write, I see a telephone. Is that just a word that someone made up out of whole cloth? No. It is composed of two Greek words: *tele* and *phone*. The first means "at a distance, from afar," while the second means "sound." Thus, a telephone is that instrument that allows you to listen to someone speaking from afar. That is how it is with much of our speech.

Because people like to "envision" what we are talking about, picturesque, or concrete terms ought to predominate in sermons. When they do, people are more interested, learn better, and find it easier to retain what is said. Metaphors ("the moon is a silver fish swimming through a sea of clouds") are an attempt to "cash in" on this dynamic. And the simile ("The kingdom of heaven is like …") grows out of a similar[2] concern. Just as these two devices openly utilize picture-language for these three purposes, concrete terms help in a similar fashion.

Don't Mislead

Preachers who use abstract language run the danger of misleading the listener. When a preacher says "car," that tells us nothing about what sort of car he has in mind. If, on the other hand, he says, "A shiny, new, fire-engine-red Corvette convertible," the listener can vividly visualize the car. If he merely says "car," the listener is likely to fill in the details on his own

---

1 Since preachers study Greek, they have an advantage in this matter. Indeed, some of both the concrete language and examples that they use may be found in tracing word origins. This is a fruitful field from which to gather a good harvest of each.
2 No pun intended. The fact is, both words are related.

and may come up with the image of an old, beat-up, gray Acclaim. Those obviously are two very different cars! Always consider the potential problem of misdirection through abstraction when communicating the Word.

The less a listener has to fill in the blanks, the more accurately he will tend to understand what a preacher says. If a preacher uses the word "sanctified" without explanation, some listeners might think of an instantaneous act of sanctification, while others might think of progressive sanctification. As a heading for a group of truths about Christian growth, the word "sanctification" does well; as a word by which a preacher seeks to convey biblical teaching about sanctification, it does not. Picturing the concept under metaphors of growth would perhaps be more helpful—and more precise. The bare use of the term may be specific enough for those "in the know," but not for those who need to know.

Phillips Brooks wanted to be sure that his congregation understood what he was saying when he preached. He mentions this concern, and speaks of being concrete, specific: "I shall be most likely to make myself intelligible if I speak not too generally...."[3]

Abstraction can be Deceptive

People may think that they are persuaded by abstract reasoning, but in most cases, that just isn't so. They are deceiving themselves. Being able to "mouth" the word "sanctification," for instance, isn't the same as understanding what it means. Until a listener is able to express the concept in everyday, concrete language, it is doubtful that he understands. So, wise preachers assume little listener knowledge and are careful to make truth explicit.

A pastor may want his people to understand and accept the doctrine of election. When some hear the word, they think of voting, punching holes in ballots, and hanging chads! Others understand just enough to cry, "Unfair!" If he doesn't fill in what he has in mind for them, they may be greatly confused. To explicate, he may begin by saying, "Perhaps the best way to remember what election means is to add an 's' to the front of the word, making it 'Selection.'" Then, in similar fashion, he may go on to explain the essential facts about election more fully. In doing so, he may anticipate the objection mentioned above and say something like this:

---

3   Phillips Brooks, *Selected Sermons*. Dutton and Co. (NY: 1950), p. 122.

Suppose a man had a bag of gold coins. And out of his goodness, he determined to give some of them away. No one had any rights or claims upon these coins. As he went through a crowd, he gave a coin to one, not to another, to a third, and so on. Now remember, no one deserved or had any rights to a coin. It was purely out of the goodness of his heart that he gave away any coins at all. Therefore, nobody would have the right to complain that this wasn't fair, would he?

The preacher may go on to explain that this is something like election. "But the goodness of God is far greater than that of the man in the story. Not only does no one have a right to salvation, but all deserve nothing but God's wrath!" Now this is all concrete language, and it is used to present truth in the form of a concrete example as well. Used together, concrete words and concrete examples are quite persuasive.

Concreteness Works Both Ways

There are, of course, other aspects to concreteness (or specificity). When a preacher (who ought to know better) says that to go to heaven, "You must take Jesus into your heart," his words can be quite misleading. Children in the congregation who think of this literally will be confused. It would be better to use a simile in which he would say, "Believing in Jesus is like …" To say that it is like trusting your mother or depending on the word of a good friend who will not let you down might be closer to the truth. But, even so, "trusting Jesus"—as well as "taking Him into your heart"—does not explain how one is saved. It omits the cross and the resurrection, which are at the very heart of the Gospel.[4] So, concreteness can cut both ways, especially when there has not been enough thought given to the implications of what one is saying. It is essential, then, to see that neither your concrete language nor your concrete illustrations leads people astray. Too often, when they do, it is because of a failure to take enough care about the matter during sermon preparation. Because of the power of specificity, it is dangerous to use concreteness carelessly or casually.

---

4 Gospel is another word that needs explanation. Preachers should point out that the word means "good news." They may make a point of the fact that "news" is about a past event that has taken place and not about some act that a person must perform in the future. Trusting Jesus means to believe and depend upon Him as the Savior Who died for one's sins and was raised from the dead by the Father, proving that his sacrifice was accepted.

Making the Abstract Persuasive

Think for a moment about the effects of concreteness upon persuasion. When a preacher says, "The Bible teaches that you can change, even if you think that you can't," he is speaking the truth. But listeners who have struggled with sin in their lives for some time don't think so. If, however, he goes on to give examples of persons on drugs who changed, marriages that were repaired by acting biblically, and people who were depressed but eventually came out of it, he will be more persuasive.[5] So, concreteness does not merely have to do with the use of words; it is also *showing* that it is possible to follow abstract truth in real life. We have seen that in Titus 1:1-2, Paul makes it plain that truth leads to life. People are rarely persuaded until they can see it demonstrated. Perhaps this isn't how it ought to be, but it is a fact that every preacher should take into consideration. It is, however, akin to the emphasis found in James, where he says that he will believe that a person has faith when he sees his works.

But, again, it is not only when an abstract truth becomes a reality for the listener as he learns that others have been able to put that truth to work in practical ways, concreteness is also important in helping people learn *how* to do so: "You see, it isn't impossible for you to be able to deal with your sinful anger. If you follow Paul's directions in Ephesians 4 to use anger constructively, you will be able to do so. Let me explain in detail what that involves. First …" Providing concrete, how-to material can make all the difference. When a person sees how to accomplish something, he is more likely to attempt to do it. Moreover, if the "how-to" is precise and detailed enough, he is not as likely to fail. Left to his own devices, he might fumble about and eventually become discouraged. In Luke 3, John's directions to those who came asking about how to work out their repentance is a good example. They could go home that day and begin to do something concrete.

Taking Care

Finally, it is essential to use concrete language correctly. There are preachers who, in attempting to do so, jumble things up. For instance, they mix metaphors. "You need to get on the ball and start rowing hard the other way"

---

[5] Of course, he will give no names and erase all identifying features about individuals and situations—unless the person specifically gives permission. In such cases that fact should be mentioned.

is an example of what I am referring to. Mixing baseball with rowing a boat is not only confusing, but since it calls attention to itself, it also detracts from the message. Whenever your words, examples, or phrases are askew, this tends to overshadow all else ("What on earth did he mean by that?"). And that can have devastating effects.

So, take time to think things through. And here is a concrete suggestion: in ordinary day-to-day talking, think about the language that you are using. Don't take the easy way out. When others are just "jawing," you ought to be working on what you will say and how you will say it. Notice also the effects of your speech on others. Revise, revise, revise—and then revise some more! Continue until you get it right. When your everyday speech improves, that improvement will carry over into your preaching. You can only do so much at a time. If you are concentrating on content and how the congregation is responding while preaching, that is enough. You don't need to give attention to how well your speech expresses your thoughts. That is why it is important to *cultivate* concreteness in all of your speech.

Chapter Nine
Conversation

Right off, let me counter any ideas of unprepared, careless, stumbling speech that is "off the cuff." That isn't what I mean by "conversational" preaching. No. Preaching must be of the highest level—but at the same time conversational. The two ideals are not contradictory. Now, what do I mean by "conversational preaching?" Listeners immediately understand good conversational preaching, and it doesn't call attention to itself because it is speech that they are used to hearing all of the time. That makes it important to examine what is involved in such preaching. It in no way differs from everyday speech that one listens to all of the time from better speakers around him. There is nothing casual or slovenly about such speech.

Conversational speech in the pulpit is free from sound, terminology, and phraseology that differ from common speech. When someone says, "He sounds like a preacher," that probably should not be taken as a compliment. A preacher should shun the stained glass voice, speaking words enshrined with halos, if he wishes to persuade people today. When one's speech calls attention to itself (as that sort of speech does), it detracts from God's message. And *that* is what the faithful preacher knows he must never do. God's message is all-important. Why preachers develop such "Pulpit-speech" is difficult to understand. Perhaps they think that it adds to their authority. But usually it does the opposite. Stiff formality makes it difficult to preach effectively about hell or, for that matter, about God's love. When a man never uses a contraction in his sermon, he will sound like a book. But that's not preaching!

What is Involved

Cultivating conversational speech is not all that difficult. After all, in some sense, you already do it. As you carry out life's activities, you can't avoid talking. And, you do it more or less by conversational speech of one sort or another. Most ministers have little difficulty carrying on reasonably intelligent conversations. In conversational speaking they will use the very same type of speech, slightly heightened by the nature of the subject matter.

So far as voice, pronunciation, word choices, and phraseology are concerned, a preacher must become proficient enough in conversational speaking to be hired by any of the networks. That means his speech would be correct grammatically and, in all other respects, a notch above average as well. It would be a fit vehicle for the message that it carries. Speech like that is not "off-hand" or filled with colloquialisms. That is the opposite of what I am talking about. Searching for words and ending up with those that don't accurately or fully communicate a thought is certainly not good conversational preaching. Speaking out of a severely limited vocabulary, in which unnecessary repetition is the rule, will hardly do. And the same may be said for humdrum, singsong speech. Such things are foreign to how a preacher should express himself in the pulpit. Instead, he should comfortably use speech that has been cultivated in everyday circumstances by the hard work that I described at the conclusion of the last chapter.

Extraordinarily Difficult?

Except for lots of practice, what does it take to cultivate a good conversational style? Well, more than reading the Puritans! We neither preach nor prepare sermons like theirs. The style that was acceptable for them surely isn't today. Not only was it stilted, but, of course, much of the language is obsolete. Many of the poor practices that may be noted in our time go back to them. Those who imitate the Puritans make a great mistake.

Think for a moment—how good were those early preachers anyway? Haven't we set them up on a pedestal? True, they preached according to the standards of the day. But that was because they set the standards! The only speech that people heard regularly came from the pulpit. For that reason, it simply didn't have to be as good as what is required today. How come?

Today, the preacher no longer sets the standard. Others do, and he must at least measure up to the standards that they set. In contrast to previous times, today we are immersed in a sea of speech. I don't have to describe how electronic communication has changed things. So, if the preacher no longer sets the standards, who does? Like it or not, it's the TV anchors, journalists, and reporters who do. In terms of sheer communication, their speech communicates quite well. It certainly rises above the speech of the average speaker. To be effective, therefore, modern preachers must measure up to present-day standards. Otherwise, a preacher will contrast unfavorably with others. And when that happens, his speech will reflect unfavorably upon God's truth.

Something to Avoid

In times past, oratorical prowess was the goal of many speakers—preachers included. They would attempt to impress listeners by the breadth of their oratorical abilities. One would seek to outdo the rest. They used long, periodic sentences in the grand style. They sought to be sensational with their extravagant terminology and purposeful prose. Those days are gone—hopefully forever! Oratory was contrived speech rather than conversational speech. It was florid. But we don't live at a time when oratorical flourishes are appreciated. The preacher who attempts to be oratorical is making a mistake for which he—and more importantly, his message—will suffer.

An Example

You probably wouldn't expect it of an accomplished Greek scholar and extraordinary theologian, but one of the greatest examples of good conversational preaching may be found in J. Gresham Machen. Consider the following passage (which is typical):

> In reply, I just want to say that I do not think that if I adopted that method I should be treating you quite fairly. Here we are, sitting down together quietly. Cannot we at least be friends? Cannot we at least try to understand each other, whether we can agree with each other or not? I do not think that I should be doing my part toward that mutual understanding if I concealed from you the real basis of what I am going to say. Hence, I am going to tell you at once, and as plainly as I can, what I think about the inspiration of the Bible. As I do that, I am afraid I shall have to relinquish any ambitions of being brilliant or sparkling or eloquent.[1]

Here is another quotation from the same seminary preacher: "I say, hold on there, brother; what is it that you said?"[2] And, he goes on to explain.

---

[1] J. Gresham Machen, *The Christian Faith in the Modern World*. Eerdmans (Grand Rapids:1936), p. 34.
[2] Ibid., p. 41.

A Forgotten Factor

The use of contractions helps. In ordinary conversation you use them all of the time, don't you? They are the very hallmark of conversational speaking. Instead of saying "it is" in many places it would be more appropriate to say "it's." The contraction enables speech to move along smoothly, avoiding many of the bumps that are found in the path of formal speech. Let's consider the following two sentences:

- Brethren, it is of the utmost importance to know that the coming of Jesus, though not imminent, is always impending.
- Brothers, it's very important for you to know that Jesus' coming, though impending, isn't imminent.

The contractions in the second sentence, together with some less formal words and phrasing, make it sound more conversational than the first. Modern ears respond more readily to language like that because it's conversational. And the use of contractions goes a long way toward making it so. Therefore, consider them "of utmost importance."

Choosing Conversationally

Notice, in the former sentences, different words and phrases were used to say the same thing. So, there are always choices to make about how we communicate what we want to say. Those choices often make the difference between conversational speech and something else. Learn to choose conversationally minded. "Brothers" is the modern word, not "brethren." Instead of saying "the coming of Jesus," say "Jesus' coming." The abstract and formal phrase "of the utmost importance" was supplanted by "very important for you to know." In the first sentence, the reader was not addressed directly; in the second, the speaker urges him to recognize the importance of the fact for himself. And that's the sort of thing that good preachers think about and cultivate by hard work.

I might mention other elements of conversational speech, but, as in previous chapters, my goal has been to avoid inundating you with too much data in favor of a few crucial matters. If you work at improving along the lines I have outlined in this chapter (and the rest of the book), you'll go a long way toward becoming a conversational preacher.

Chapter Ten
Conciseness

In ordinary conversations, there are people who bore you by going on and on and on, talking about something that interests them, but hardly anyone else. They never know when to stop. When it appears they are about to cross the finish line, they suddenly remember some "little detail" that just must be "mentioned" or are reminded of an event akin to the one that they have been discoursing. At that point, you are about ready to tear your hair out! Well, if that's bad in everyday conversation—where you can always attempt to interrupt or, looking at your watch depart for safer territory saying, "I must go now"—think how bad it is for a person sitting in the pew who doesn't have those options.

Conciseness, or brevity, is a virtue to be pursued by the preacher who wants to persuade. No one offers a better example of brevity than Jesus. His metaphors, similes, and examples are always simple, to the point, and concise. It did not take a myriad of detail to make those points. In contrast, there are those who make their point, and even possibly are on the verge of persuading the congregation, but then turn them off by numerous repetitions or endless discourse. More than once, I have listened to a well-known minister who, in the opening portions of his sermon, usually has something worthwhile to say, and it looks like he is going to convince us of it. But then he adds two or three conclusions to his sermon, during which time he loses his congregation. It seems that he is about to win the race when he puts his car in reverse and begins his conclusion all over again. The problem is, there are always several things that he remembers that he simply "must" say before closing the message. If he had planned better ahead of time, this wouldn't happen.

But There's So Much to Say

Yes, of course there is. You will never be able to exhaust biblical teaching. And it's true that one thing often reminds you of another because everything is interrelated. That too is true. But you can not say it all at once. And you must resist the temptation to spread out to other areas of thought. Even apostles, whose writings were inspired, were not able to do so. So, out of the limitless range of revealed facts, they chose those that were best suited to the occasion and to the ability of the reader to comprehend.

Don't Be Egged On

There are those who object, "But you didn't mention …" Of course, you didn't. But neither did the biblical writer in the passage you are expositing. "Take your objection to him!" If you were to satisfy such persons, it would take you all day to interrelate every truth that has any bearing on others in order to satisfy them. Meanwhile, the rest of the congregation will have departed. It is impossible to deal with every aspect of every truth in a sermon. It is time for many preachers to learn that. When others demand such *comprehensive* depth and breadth in a sermon, remind them that it took 66 books called the Bible to teach all that is necessary for life and godliness. Surely, then, God didn't intend a preacher to cover everything in one sermon!

You May Be the Problem

But it isn't only others who may demand more than can be stuffed into one sermon; most likely, the culprit who makes the attempt is the preacher himself. It is important for him to determine how much he can preach in any given sermon as well as how much the congregation can take in during that time. But how can he make such a determination? A preaching portion should contain one telos, as I have shown in my book, *Preaching with Purpose*. A telic unit is a preaching portion that has a purpose. It is a unit of truth given by the Holy Spirit to make some change in the thinking, beliefs, attitudes, and actions of those who hear. That, then, is the amount of material that a sermon should contain. There will be other opportunities to preach on other aspects of the matter being considered. Waiting till then allows the preacher to treat each aspect of teaching more fully, both at this point and later on.

And, as I said, the ability of the congregation to absorb and implement what you want to say will determine how deeply you treat the subject. The writer to the Hebrews concluded, "We have a lot to say about this, but it is hard to explain since you have become dull of hearing" (Hebrews 5:11). People are not persuaded by the bulk of material you cover, but by the way you treat the material that you do present. Preached clearly, cogently, and in a conversational manner, less material will always trump bulk.

Advice About This

Earlier in this book, I suggested revise and revise and then revise some more. Now, I'd like to add to that—cut and cut and then cut some more. Trim off all of the fat. A lean sermon, well marbled, like a quality cut of meat, is what you want. To change the analogy, all "padding" should be on the seats of the pews, not in the sermon that those who sit on them must listen to.

How do you know what to cut? As you look at the message before you in the study, ask some questions about the various elements in it.

- Is this element really necessary?
- Could I say this in a more concise way—perhaps by using a memorable phrase?
- Am I simply trying to spice up the message by including this item?
- How much detail is really required to make this point?
- Does my reasoning stand out clearly (we might even say starkly), or is it covered up with extraneous material?
- Could more, briefer material be used to build up my arguments? Adding can be subtracting.
- Am I remembering that "you can say more about less?"
- Who in the congregation needs to hear what; who doesn't? Is everything going to be useful to everyone?
- Do I need to slow down and preach a series of messages about this since my congregation may lack the necessary background knowledge to digest it?
- Is the message focused on the *telos* in the preaching portion, or am I about to wander away from it?
- Does the conclusion of the sermon end up where the introduction said it was going to go?
- Is my language wordy rather than precise?

Obviously, these are but starters. Any number of other questions might also be asked. If there are one or two questions that especially pertain to your preaching, be sure that you ask them every week as you prepare. Admit and remember your weaknesses and ask God to help as you work on them. There is no other way to improve. But …

Don't develop a brevity fetish. You can err both ways. Be sure that every argument necessary to persuade is included. Be certain that you have taken the time to fully exposit the passage and explain everything that may be difficult to comprehend. An illustration may be necessary at some point to clarify or demonstrate how something can be done, even though it takes a bit of time away from something else. When assigning a paper as a professor in two seminaries, some students would always ask, "How long should it be?" My stock answer was, "Long enough to do the job and short enough that I won't be bored reading it." In other words, all that is necessary should be included—and no more. Conciseness, when one's preaching is "tight," in itself lends force to what he says. It correctly gives the appearance of having thought a matter through. And, since one is able to present it in concise form, the logic of an argument stands out more sharply. Take time to give a lot of attention to this issue.

Chapter Eleven
Conclusion

"It is the part of an ambassador to enforce by argument what he brings forward in the name of his prince."[1]

If you believe this, by all means you will want to be a faithful ambassador for Christ who uses all of the legitimate, biblical means available to "enforce" His messages to the world and to His people. As Calvin said, this will happen when he successfully "argues" his case. Of course, the word argument is used here in the positive sense of the term. Indeed, proper argumentation—as I show here—is contrary to argumentativeness.

I have not endeavored to lay out the principles of argumentation or reasoning. That is far more than I intended to do. But as you have seen, the goal was to help the reader think through those elements that have to do with the *language* of persuasion. To that end I have tried to set forth, from a number of angles, those desirable preaching practices that, from the preacher's perspective on his language, enhance his reasoning. As you have seen, there is much in how an argument for truth is set forth by the preacher that will hinder rather than enhance it. And conversely, there are ways of presenting an argument that will "enforce" it. It is those matters that I have attempted to visit. I have not spelled out exhaustively all that one might do to make his language more persuasive. Some things in the book are suggestive, pointing in a direction that the reader may explore further on his own. On the other hand, much more is instructive, providing direction that, when properly applied, should make his preaching more persuasive. I assume that the reader has been able to distinguish between the two.

Since preachers use language as the means by which they proclaim God's truth, they cannot avoid consideration of the use of language. Since

---
1 John Calvin, *Commentaries*, vol. 20, p. 244.

persuasion is so much a part of their task, neither can they avoid thinking about the language they use to persuade. To avoid either is perilous to the preacher. Indeed, it is nothing short of failure to faithfully carry out the task given to him by God.

Now, if I have not yet made it clear, let me do so now. It is neither the preacher nor his language that, in the final analysis, persuades anyone. It is the Spirit of God Who changes both their thinking and their actions. Yet, there are two facts to remember: 1) God calls us to be faithful stewards of the gifts He gave us. We must fully consider how to improve our use of them. Paul wrote, "pay attention to the public reading of Scripture, to exhortation, to teaching. Don't neglect the gift that is in you.... Practice these things; be fully involved in them so that your progress may be apparent to everybody" (1 Timothy 4:13-16). The word "progress" (*prokope*) means "to move forward into new territory." Thus, Paul calls for attention to matters that may not have been explored previously. It is possible that what you have read here, at least in part, is like that. I hope that if that is so, having read this book will move you forward to conquer that new territory.

I have made every effort to make the book practical, but I have not filled it with stories, examples, and the like. I don't know about you, but when I take up a book like that, I find myself skimming over such appetizers to try to get to the "meat and potatoes" as quickly as possible. Preachers are busy people. They need to go to the heart of things. They have little time for purely interesting reading. They need those helps that they may immediately put into practice. I have tried to write with that end in view. May He help you through what you have read to become a more persuasive ambassador for Christ!

Preaching With Parables

Introduction

Have you ever thought about preaching in parables? "Me?" you ask. "Preach parables?" Why not? Have you got a good reason? "Well …" If not, then think about it. You know, of course, that Jesus preached with parables; indeed, one third of His recorded preaching is parabolic! Why shouldn't you? If you have never done so, perhaps you (and your congregation) have been missing out on something important.

Do your sermons lack a penetrating quality that elicits response? Do people leave the church perfunctorily saying "Nice sermon, pastor," but never show that what they heard affects them very much? Could preaching parables change that—could it make a significant difference?

Suppose you did want to use parables—would you know where to begin and how to construct them? Do you know where to find the ideas and other materials with which to do it? What is a parable, anyway? Why and when should they be used—and for what purposes? How would you go about introducing parables into sermons? These are questions that you ought to be able to answer. And, in this book, I have endeavored to answer them—and more—according to a simple, easily followed plan, together with directions about what to do—from start to finish.

If the idea of preaching in parables is entirely new to you, then open your mind and give it some thought. In this book, you may find just what you have been looking for. Something to make your preaching come alive. Something it now lacks. It may point to the road that will lead you to more helpful biblical preaching than you or your congregation has experienced before. You might begin like this:

> A certain man went into a restaurant to eat. The tablecloth was soiled, and the waiter could not explain anything on the menu. After waiting an inordinate amount of time for his dinner, the man was served inedible food. Obviously, the chef did not know how to cook or season steak. What was offered was a raw slab of meat. The potatoes were burned to a crisp, and the dessert was an unidentifiable, indigestible

conglomeration of what appeared to be leftover sweets. Disgusted, the customer went away hungry.

What do you suppose the owner of the restaurant will do when he hears what happened?

Chapter One
From Proverb to Parable

Jesus enhanced His preaching with parables, but most preachers today do not. This lack may contribute to the failure of much modern preaching. That there is such a failure is apparent—even to preachers themselves. When teaching in the doctoral homiletics program at Westminster Seminary in California, I often asked ministers what they thought of today's preaching. Their answers were always strongly negative. Then I asked further, "What causes do you attribute to this poor showing?" They would go on for the better portion of that hour listing items. Many of these were quite insightful, and during the days of the course that followed, I would address most of them. But, curiously, in teaching that class for ten years, no one ever suggested, "I think we should learn to preach with parables like Jesus did." The thought was far from their thinking, as it had been from mine until I began to consider the matter. If polled, I believe that to a man they would agree that in their undergraduate preaching courses, the idea was never broached. It seems, therefore, desirable to do something about the matter.

Children from nine to ninety-nine like stories. Though more than that, a parable is a story.[1] You know that when the preacher begins to tell a story interest picks up among the members of the congregation. Heads are raised, eyes brighten, and even the young people pay attention. Mark tells us that the large crowds which followed Jesus "heard Him with pleasure" (Mark 12:37). Could it not have been that one reason for their enthusiasm was Jesus' frequent use of figures of speech, proverbs, and parables?

At any rate, the goal of this book is to help you learn and master the art of telling parables. Once you catch on, the task comes readily. You will find yourself at first looking for parabolic material, but later on, seeing such material all around you—without looking. It will become a habit of

---

[1] It is a particular kind of story, with a special purpose, as we shall see later in the book.

observation. "But where does one look? And how does he go about it?" you ask. The answers to these and other questions will be found in subsequent chapters.

For now, however, I want to suggest one of the answers: a good way to begin to construct parables is to move from proverb to parable. As you read, I think you will agree that this is a natural thing to do. In fact, there is reason to believe that on at least one occasion, that is precisely what Jesus did. In His most famous sermon—the one that we call The Sermon on the Mount—He did not conclude weakly as many preachers do when they say, "Now, may God bless this to each and every one of you" (or words to that effect). No. He concluded with a parable—the parable of the two foundations. The man who built his house on a foundation of sand lost everything when the winds and the waves beat upon it; the man who built on the rock found that his house weathered the storm. Jesus made it clear that the first man is like those who hear His words and does not do them, while the second man is like those who hear His words and do them (Matthew 7:24). To meet the vicissitudes of life, one must stand firmly upon God's Word and live according to it.

Now, compare Proverbs 10:25: "When the storm passes, the wicked are not, but the righteous has an enduring foundation." Notice the parallels: a storm, two foundations, the contrast of wicked and righteous persons, and the opposite outcomes. While no one can be sure that Jesus expanded this proverb into a parable (He may have received a mere suggestion from it), it is likely that He did. At any rate, I think you can see that if you were to flesh out the principle set forth in this picture-proverb, the resultant parable would look very much like the one that Jesus told. Obviously, then, there is fertile ground for harvesting parables from among the tender sprouts found in the book of Proverbs.

Chapter Two
What the Words Tell Us

There is but one Hebrew word that is used to designate both a parable and a proverb: *mashal*. This interesting phenomenon itself should cause us to associate the two closely. This word denotes some sort of "likeness" or "comparison."[1] It seems plain that in not distinguishing the parable from the proverb (as we too readily do), the Hebrews saw no sharp difference between them. In modern times, the tendency to separate them has led to some confusion among those who write books about parables. The writers do not always agree on the number of parables since they find it difficult to determine what a parable is. G. Campbell Morgan solved the problem by entitling his book, *The Parables and Metaphors of Our Lord*. Under this title, he covered the whole territory! Since there is no hard distinction between the two, it is easy to see how one might shade off into the other.

In the Greek New Testament there are two terms that have been translated "parable." The first is *parabole* which, obviously, is the source of our word "parable." The term literally means "a throwing alongside of" and indicates that a story is used to convey a parallel or analogous truth. Someone has quaintly called the parable "An earthly story with a heavenly meaning." While that explanation doesn't quite say all that might be said, it does show that the parable exists not for its own sake, but in order to teach something else. It is possible for it to be used for teaching truth because something (usually not everything) in the parable is analogous to that truth.[2]

The other term is *paroimia*. While close to the former term, nevertheless, it designates something somewhat different from *parabole*. The *paroimia* is close to what we call an *Obiter Dictum*. It refers to "something by the way." That is to say, it is something *alongside* something else. Perhaps the

---
1 The old root of the word *mashal* is "shadow." As the shadow corresponds to the reality, so a parable corresponds to a message.
2 When more than one aspect of the "parable" is analogous, we call the resultant story an "allegory."

closest modern example is the side-bar that appears along with the text of a published article. This side-bar highlights something especially significant in the straightforward material it accompanies. It tends to make the listener (reader) stop and think about something that he might otherwise allow to slip by him. This second word is used by John and Peter, whereas other writers use the former. This figure of speech is seen in John 10:6, for instance. Here Jesus refers back to the saying in verses 1 through 5. The saying was left hanging for the listener to consider. But because the disciples did not understand, Jesus went on to explain its meaning. Clearly, the disciples came to realize later on the difference between the *paroimia* and ordinary narrative. They were able to understand the intended contrast between ordinary and figurative speech: "His disciples said, We see! Now you are speaking plainly and not speaking figuratively" (John 16:29). They took their clue from Jesus who first contrasted plain speech (*parresia*) with figurative speech (*paroimia*). This contrast points up the fact that the *paroimia* is a byword to the straightforward material that is found in the narrative.

Chapter Three
A Special Sort of Story

We have seen that a parable is a story. Yet, not every story is a parable. What makes the difference? The stories that qualify as parables are shaped so as to convey a parallel principle or truth. That is to say, they are composed of elements that, when properly combined, set forth principles and truths under the form of a story. The story has no value in itself; it is a means to an end. It is but a vehicle.

The story of creation in Genesis, for instance, is not a parable. To tell the story of the mustard seed, however, is to tell a parable. The former is a straightforward historical narrative. There is nothing more to be understood than what is said. This sort of discourse is what Jesus and the disciples referred to as *parresia* or "plain speaking." In contrast, the story of the mustard seed is not history. It is also not told to inform the listener about the growth of mustard seeds. Rather, it is told in order to show how the kingdom of God, even though it had a small, fragile beginning, would grow into something large and substantial. The details of the mustard seed example exist only for the sake of the underlying, parallel, or analogous truth. A parable, therefore, may be said to be a story with a message. The message is not direct and may seem hidden. But it is this significant thing about a parable that the listener is supposed to uncover.

Now, not all the details of a parable are to be pressed as containing truth in themselves. Often, it is only the story as a whole that conveys the truth. In other words, elements of the parable may be present merely because they are necessary to make a coherent story. The prodigal son feeding pigs is, of course, intended to show to what depths he descended. But the story is not about that. As we shall see in the next chapter, the purpose of that parable lies elsewhere. In seeking to interpret a parable, one must discover the intent of the speaker in telling it. The intent is not to teach us anything about prodigals and pigs, as such, or what they might "stand for."

So the parable is a story with a point. Nathan did not tell David a parable to instruct him about lambs but to awaken David to his great sin in order to bring him to repentance. And, as David himself tells us in Psalm 51, it effectively achieved that purpose. The withered fig tree had nothing to do with agriculture or the time of the year when figs are ripe. Jesus was making the point that, like the fig tree which bore no fruit, Israel would be cursed and die as a nation. Because a parable is a story with a purpose, its author always has an ulterior motive in telling it.

Notice also that all parables have to do with real life. In Jesus' parables, He depicts people doing everyday activities. He also uses normal objects of life, such as leaven and trees. In contrast to the fable, in which animals talk and people do impossible things (like turning princes into frogs), the parable is always true to life. The parable does not detract from the message it brings by adding all sorts of extraneous material—especially of the fabulous sort.

In one of Jesus' parables, it seems certain that he referred to a contemporary event that all knew about (Luke 19:12ff).[1] So, we see, parables were not always (probably not even ordinarily) expanded proverbs. Why then use proverbs as the inspiration for constructing parables? The answer is that the proverbs, in the Old Testament book that bears that name, provide a good starting point for the novice. In expanding and enlarging upon the many pictures in the book of Proverbs that are attached to a truth or principle, one may more readily learn to develop parables.

One of the most difficult tasks for the beginner is to determine what truths to "parabolize," and how to attach to them a storyline that will enable him to get his point across. Using a proverb, which is already a sort of miniature parable, helps solve those problems. Many of the proverbs are mini-pictures that readily lend themselves to expansion. Because these picture-proverbs are intended to stimulate the reader's thought, they may also serve the additional purpose of enabling the preacher to carry out that thought to a greater extent. Hence, the parable. Proverbs covers a wide range of human experiences, which also adds to the variety one would desire in constructing parables. You do not want all of them to be similar or stress the same point unless you have a reason for doing so. Finally, the proverbs are important and correct or they would not be a part of God's Word.

---

[1] Archelaus went to Rome to receive a mini kingdom from the emperor; an event that required a long absence before he returned.

One caution: don't restrict your expansion of a proverb to those exact elements that appear in the proverb. Jesus spoke about items that pertained to the life of those around Him that were familiar to them at the time. He led them from the known to the unknown. So let your parables do the same thing; always be contemporary. While taking a tour to Palestine in your exegesis, preach while standing on American soil.

Chapter Four
Let's Take One Apart

Now that we have looked at some aspects of the parable, I want to take a hard look at one parable in order to illustrate more fully those facts that we have considered. It is one thing to speak abstractly about a matter; it is another to dig in and demonstrate the abstract principles.[1] The parable in view is found in Luke 15. Have you ever referred to that chapter as the "Lost and Found Chapter" as so many do? Well, if you have, by the time I am through with an analysis of it, I hope you will never do so again.

"What?" you say. "Isn't that what the chapter is all about—a lost sheep, a lost coin, and a lost son which are found?" Sure, Jesus speaks about each of those things, but placing emphasis on that which is lost and that which is found—as if that dynamic were the point of the parable—is a fallacy of the first order. "Well, then, tell me what the point is." All in good time. First, let's look at the parable.

> *Now the tax collectors and sinners were coming near to listen to Him. But the Pharisees and the scribes grumbled, saying, "This person welcomes sinners and eats with them." So He told them this parable:*
>
> *Which one of you people, if he had a hundred sheep and had lost one of them, wouldn't leave the ninety-nine in the desert and search for the lost sheep until he finds it? Then, when he finds it, he puts it on his shoulders, rejoicing. When he comes home, he calls his friend and neighbors together and says to them, "Rejoice with me! I have found my sheep that was lost." I tell you that in just that way there will be more joy in heaven over one sinner who repents than over ninety-nine righteous persons who have no need for repentance.*

---

1 Incidentally, the parable serves that very purpose. Rather than throw principles at people, Jesus demonstrated how those principles play out in actual experience, how they clarify or cloud the listener's understanding.

> Or what woman who has ten silver coins, if she loses one, doesn't light a lamp and sweep the house and carefully look for it until she finds it? Then when she finds it, she calls together those women who are her friends and neighbors and says, "Rejoice with me! I found the silver coin that I lost." I tell you that in just that way, there is joy in the presence of God's angels over one sinner who repents.

And He continued,

> A certain man had two sons. The younger said to his father, "Father, give me my share of the property that is coming to me." So he divided his possessions between them. Now it wasn't long before the younger son gathered together everything he owned and left for a country far away. And there he squandered his possessions in wild living. When he had spent everything, there was a bad famine throughout that country, and he began to be in need. So he went out and got a job with a citizen of that country, who sent him into his field to feed pigs. And he longed to fill his stomach with the pods that the pigs were eating, but nobody gave him anything. But when he came to himself, he said, "How many of my father's hired servants have more than enough bread, while I am perishing here in this famine! I'm going to get up and go to my father and say to him, 'Father, I sinned against heaven and before you. I am no longer worthy to be called your son. Treat me as one of your hired servants.'" So he got up and went away to his father.
> Now while he was still at a distance his father saw him and was moved with compassion for him. So he ran to him and hugged and kissed him. But the son said to him, "Father, I have sinned against heaven and before you. I am no longer worthy to be called your son ..." But the father said to his slaves, "Quickly, bring out the best robe and clothe him. And put a ring on his hand and sandals on his feet, and bring the fattened calf and slaughter it, and let us eat and celebrate. This son of mine was dead and is alive again; he was lost and is found." So they began to celebrate.
> Now the older son was in the field, and as he came in and drew near to the house he heard music and dancing. So he called one of the servants and asked him what was happening. So he said to him, "Your brother has come and your father killed the fattened calf because he has returned safe and sound." Then he grew angry and didn't want to go in. So his father went out and

> *begged him. But he answered, "Think of it! For so many years I have served you like a slave, and never disobeyed a command of yours, but you never even gave me a goat so that I could celebrate with my friends. But when this son of yours, who has devoured your possessions with prostitutes, returned, you killed the fattened calf for him."*
>
> *Then he replied, "Son, you are always with me; so everything that I have is yours. It was right for us to celebrate and rejoice, because this brother of yours was dead and is alive again; he was lost and is found."*

Now, think about what you have just read. Is the fact of that which is lost and found the main point that Jesus is making? Certainly, all through the story you read of something lost and something found. But why did Jesus tell this parable? What was His purpose in doing so? How did He expect those who listened to respond?

Many, perhaps most, preachers think of this as an opportunity to preach a gospel message (or three). But while the passage certainly alludes to the gospel and the salvation of the lost, it was not Jesus' purpose to provide material for preaching an evangelistic message.[2] Look at the first two verses of the chapter. In them, the setting and occasion for the parable are clearly spelled out. Pharisees and scribes were grousing about the fact that Jesus was associating with tax collectors and notorious sinners. Then, in verse three we read, "So He told them this parable."[3] It was a response to their complaints.

To miss the thrust of the parable is to misinterpret it. And, in turn, that will lead to misapplying it in preaching. Jesus' concern is to counter the hard, self-righteous attitude of the Pharisees and scribes. That, plainly, is the reason for the parable. And in conjunction with that insight, why not change the heading from The Lost and Found Chapter to The Lost, SEARCHED FOR and found, and REJOICED OVER chapter? While not so euphonious, that puts the emphasis where it ought to be.

Do you see that? Jesus shows how the shepherd gathered together his friends and *rejoiced* over the sheep that was found. The same is true of the

---

2   Certainly, in preaching from this passage you will want to present the gospel—as you should in every message. But the message of salvation is really a sub-theme. Those preachers who turn the chapter into a text primarily for proclaiming the message of salvation, miss the point altogether.

3   Clearly, there is but one parable here—not three. Jesus speaks of "this parable," not "these parables." What we have is a three-part parable with a "kicker" at the end.

woman and the father. And notice how that comes about—the shepherd, the woman, and the father are searching for that which is lost. Jesus was searching out tax collectors and notorious sinners to save, and the angels in heaven rejoiced when one who was dead came to life spiritually. But the religious leaders were like the elder brother who was complaining about Jesus spending time with the lost in order to bring them into the fold.

Notice how this one parable unfolds. The sheep is lost, searched for, and rejoiced over. Everyone shakes his head and says, "Yes, that's what true shepherds do." Then, they respond similarly to the tale of the rejoicing woman and the father who rejoiced over the return of his wayward son. "Yes, yes, yes" is the way that the listener would respond, nodding his head in agreement. But then, completely out of sync with those responses, there is the response of the elder brother. Through this parable, Jesus charged the insensitive religious leaders with an attitude like that brother.

Now that we know the intention of the Holy Spirit in recording this parable of Jesus through Luke, we shall look more closely at it. There is no doubt that this is a marvelous parable. It has great force in making its point. It builds to the climax in which the elder son's sinful attitude is highlighted, and concludes with a brief statement of the father in which he makes the point: "It was right to celebrate and rejoice (v. 32)." That is to say, contrary to the way everyone in the parable responded by rejoicing, the religious leaders' response was wrong. Surely, in making this summary statement, Jesus was setting forth the need for these leaders themselves to come to repentance, just as the elder brother should. In preaching, it should be used to rebuke self-righteous members of the congregation who are adverse to the evangelism of disreputable persons.

A motorcycle gang—for whatever reason—decides to attend service at your church en masse. They file down the aisle, scraping the cleats on their boots across your newly refinished floor. They scrape their metal-studded belts against your newly varnished pews as they wriggle from the lice that are running up and down their backs from their stringy hair (which, incidentally, streams down on the hymn books in the pew rack behind them). Like the scribes and Pharisees, people begin to grumble: "Did you ever? Why don't they attend church on the other side of the railroad tracks!" It is then that the full force of the parable can be brought home by the preacher—if he has the courage to preach it for the purpose for which it was given! Next week he has his text! Instead of their response, the congregation should rejoice, reach out to the gang, and seek to win them to the Lord. If any of them get saved, you can rejoice and (if you think it is appropriate) hold a party at which they join in refinishing the floor and pews!

Now, look at the parable itself. There are all sorts of details that some have attempted to interpret allegorically. The pertinent question that reveals this allegorical mentality is "What does this stand for?" Some find significance in the shepherd carrying his sheep across his shoulders: Some think that the ninety-nine sheep "stand for" something. How about the woman's coin—and what about the light she lights to search? Then, there are the neighbors, friends, and women who gather together to rejoice with the main characters in the story. And what about those pigs that I mentioned earlier—and the pods and the famine and the far country? What do they stand for?

The answer, of course, is that these elements are given in order to make the parable come alive. Notice how important dialogue is—Jesus has the son talking to himself and practicing exactly what he will say to his father. The famine, the pigs, and all of the rest of the incidentals, along with the dialogue, develop the parable by lending color that makes it realistic. The question "What do they stand for?" is totally inappropriate. These incidental elements don't "stand for" anything! There is one point to the parable, which is quite clearly seen in the introductory and closing words.

Think about these things and take them to heart as you interpret and preach the parables of Jesus—and, eventually, your own. Don't try to make everything "stand for" something else, but simply bring into your parable what is necessary to make it a realistic story.[4] That is the first, and one of the most important rules for creating parables.

---

[4] And no more. Don't clutter it with unnecessary details or extraneous materials or information.

Chapter Five

Becoming a Good Scribe

It is true that the scribes, along with the Pharisees, opposed Jesus' teaching. As we saw in Chapter Three, they grumbled about His evangelistic associations with sinners (immoral outcasts) and tax collectors.[1] But the office of scribe, itself, was not the thrust of our Lord's condemnation.[2] In Matthew 13, at the conclusion of the string of parables that He uttered, He asked the disciples, "Did you understand all of this?" (v. 51). They replied in the affirmative. Then, we read, "So[3] He said to them, 'Therefore every scribe discipled for the kingdom from the heavens is like a householder who brings out of his treasure new things and old things' " (vv. 51, 52).

The placing of this comment at the end of Jesus' discussion of parabolic preaching is significant. He wanted them to know something about how to speak in parables. What He was saying was that good preaching relates the unknown to the known (the new to the old). That, of course, is what He did in using parables to teach truth. The word "like" that occurs throughout the chapter in the introductions to several parables plainly shows that He used the familiar to explain the unfamiliar. He, Himself, is the prime example of the scribe who brings things both new and old from his treasure. Indeed, even in explaining His method (and that which was to be the method of every good scribe who followed in His footsteps), he did so through the use of a parable. If preaching involves bringing things old and new out of a scribe's treasure, then Jesus did that very thing by teaching about parabolic teaching by means of a parable!

What was a scribe? At first, these men were secretaries, copiers of Scripture and other documents, and were often officials of the government. By

---
1 See Matthew 23:16, etc.
2 Jesus would send forth "prophets and wise men and scribes to preach the gospel throughout the world" (Matthew 23:34). Obviously, this verse refers to the apostles and prophets.
3 This connecting word indicates that what follows grows out of what precedes.

New Testament times, however, they had also become teachers of the Old Testament *Torah*[4] (or law). This new function may have begun with—or, at least received strong impetus from—the teaching ministry carried on by Ezra the scribe in the post-exilic period (Ezra 7:6; Nehemiah 8:1-13).[5] The scribe was the theologian (or "doctor of the law") of Jesus' day, a man who also preached and taught (cf. Luke 5:17; Acts 5:34). The *Christian* scribe is the pastor-teacher (Ephesians 4:11).[6] He engages in "teaching and preaching" (1 Timothy 5:17).

When Jesus speaks of bringing things new and old out of his treasure, He pictures the owner of a house going into his house and, from a treasure box that contained his valuables, bringing out things that he had owned for a long time as well as some recent acquisitions. He then likens this scenario to His own preaching and to the preaching that He expects His disciples to engage in when they go forth to preach the gospel to the nations. He wanted them to take a cue from His use of parabolic sayings intended to make the unknown known by referring to the known.

Everyone knew about fishing, for instance. So, in the most recent parable, Jesus likens the kingdom from the heavens to what happens when the fishing net is drawn up. It brings a collection of various sorts of fish—some of which were useful, some of which were not. The good fish were saved; the worthless were thrown back. He then explains how this is just like what will take place at the final judgment (Matthew 13:49-50).[7] To explain the judgment in terms of the known and the unknown not only clarified His words but also made them memorable. Whenever a listener would watch men fishing with nets he would be reminded of Jesus' words. So, the new and the old not only clarified but served a powerful mnemonic purpose as well.

Because the parables were taken from daily life they required no explanation in themselves. The known object and its use or activity in which

---

[4] *Torah* came from a word meaning "to point the finger in order to show the way." The Old Testament was God's guide for life. Ezra became a "skillful scribe by determining to learn God's Word, practice it, and teach it to others (Ezra 7:8-10). For more on this matter, see my book, *Committed to Craftsmanship*.
[5] For an interesting discussion of the scribal office, see Sirach (*Ecclesiasticus*) 38:24-40:11.
[6] The two terms are used of only one person. They correspond to the teaching and ruling about which Paul writes to Timothy (1 Timothy 2:12).
[7] Likeness is inherent in many proverbs. Cf. The frequent use of "as" (e.g., Proverbs 25:11; 26:18, 9)

people were engaged was immediately apparent. The *unknown* was the parallel or analogous truth or principle that Jesus taught. There are preachers today who will concoct an illustration that is complex and calls attention to itself because it involves things unfamiliar. They attempt to explain the unknown by the unknown! As a result, what they say becomes a hindrance to understanding rather than an aid. By making the parable or illustration difficult to understand, they direct one's attention away from the underlying truth they wish to teach to the illustration itself. Thus, it is important for a preacher to use parabolic materials that may be instantly understood. That, of course, may differ from congregation to congregation. But it would be wise to limit one's illustrations to what is simple and easily understood by everyone—as Jesus did. While we have begun to look somewhat at the use and structure of a true parable, we must devote the next chapter to a fuller discussion of this matter. For now, get it clear—the parable is not to be so "cute," so striking, so difficult to comprehend that it thereby fails to serve its purpose. The parable's primary purpose, remember, is to convey the truth, exhortation, or principle that is associated with it. The parable exists not for its own sake, but for the sake of the parallel truth. Good scribes will understand and freely sprinkle their sermons with parables.

Chapter Six
About Proverbs

SINCE we shall be learning how to turn proverbs into parables, it is important to know something about proverbs. Scattered here and there in this volume we have mentioned in passing a number of facts concerning proverbs. It is now time to pull these together so as to gain a fuller understanding of the sources that we shall tap when making parables out of proverbs. In my commentary on the book of Proverbs,[1] I have analyzed the proverbial method. Here, I would like to give you some excerpts from the introduction:

> Proverbs is a teaching manual ... as a piece of wisdom literature, it includes *truth for* life. The ways of wisdom and the failures of folly are frequently contrasted, the proverbial form of the contrasting couplet being the principal method of constructing the comparison ... it is a book of revealed morality. It contains divine wisdom from God for His covenant people.... As the Psalms focus on *man* in relationship to *God*, the Proverbs focus on *man* in relationship to *man* ... against the backdrop of one's relationship to God ... Jesus Christ is the Wisdom of God. He it is, therefore, into Whose likeness one grows as he appropriates and incorporates Proverbs' teaching into daily living. As a result, it is a thoroughly Christian, Christ-honoring book ... often the proverbs give the result of compacting truth tightly into one unit. The process looks something like this:
>
> The writer constructed the proverb
> > out of *particulars* from which he formed a *generalization* that he applied to *one particular* in which he encapsulated the *generalization* in the form of a pithy proverb,
>
> From which, in turn, the interpreter
> > must again abstract the *generalization* behind it and then apply

---

[1] My translation of Proverbs may be found in *The Christian Counselor's Commentary* and in *The Christian Counselor's New Testament and Proverbs*.

it to that or any number of other *particular* situations to which it also validly applies.

In 1 Corinthians 9:9, you see Paul at work interpreting an Old Testament verse in exactly this way. Referring to Deuteronomy 25:4, Paul quotes a proverbial instruction about not muzzling the ox that is treading out the grain. This is the particular situation to which the generalization, that the worker should benefit (live) from his work, is applied. Paul saw the generalization behind the particular and applied it to a *different* particular: the preacher should be paid out of his work.

Why is the proverbial form, with its compactness, valuable? One major reason is that a proverb is portable truth compacted into that easily memorized, often vivid or picturesque particular situation that the proverb addresses. It is a generalization that may be readily learned, carried about in one's mind, and applied to any number of life situations as they occur.

Moreover, proverbs are thought-starters. They get you thinking along certain lines … and expect you to fill in the rest (cf., for instance, Proverbs 21:2).[2]

From the above you can see several of factors that have implications for parable-making:

- The proverbial form of the comparing and contrasting couplet lends itself to the parabolic form frequently used by the Lord. A prime example is that of the Parable of the Pharisee and the Publican (Luke 16). Other examples include the parable of the Rich man and Lazarus, the wheat and the tares, and the two foundations. Contrast is of the essence in these and other parables.

- Truth is tightly compacted in most proverbs (especially from Proverbs 10 and following). This encourages—I almost said *demands*— the parable-maker to unpack a proverb, thereby disclosing all of its contents as Paul did when discussing oxen and preachers. As the preacher explores the many ramifications of the principle behind the proverb that illustrates it, he will also find that he is able to shake out multiple possible parabolic themes.

---

2   Ibid.

- The picturesque proverb[3] attached to a principle is exactly what, in expanded form, we find in the parables. That means that the proverb is a parable ready to go! All one has to do is expand it in a contemporary manner.

More could be said about the suitability of proverbs as sources for parable-making, but certainly enough has been said here, and elsewhere in the book, to point you in the right direction.

---

[3] Some are more picturesque than others and, thus, lend themselves more readily to parable-making.

Chapter Seven
Features to Recognize

Biblical parables usually have one or more of the following characteristics:
1. Some are shocking in nature. Included in these are the parables about amputating the right eye, the right foot, and the right hand, as well as the parable about hating the members of one's family.
2. Others leave the listener/reader hanging; no resolution or conclusion is apparent. The parable of the fig tree is one example.
3. Still others have a surprise twist. The story of the elder brother and the parable of the three-year-old fig tree that didn't bear fruit both exhibit this characteristic.

All parables, as we have seen, consist of two essential elements: the tale and the truth (the story and the message). It is not necessary, however, for the tale to maintain in all respects a one-to-one relationship to the truth it conveys. Consider, for instance, how in the parable of the elder brother (see Chapter Three), the shepherd, and the woman each "searched" for something that was lost. But the father doesn't search for his lost son. Instead, we see him responding only when the son has come to his senses and returned. Because of that divergence are we to look for some special meaning? No. In keeping with the *spirit* of the searches, when the father sees the son far off, he *runs* to him. So, the correspondence of the truth and the tale lies not so much in precise likenesses between all elements of story and message, but in exactness of thought and intention. Differences may be accounted for by the necessities of the story itself. It would not have been as true to life to have the father searching, so He is said to run to the son when he appears. This divergence, therefore, makes good sense because it is the message that is all-important and the story is but the vehicle in which it travels. As long as the message is clear and not distorted, the Holy Spirit saw fit to vary the elements of the story at some points, thereby making the story more realistic.

Every parable is intended to teach some truth to those who have the ears to hear. But by the nature of the fact, those who are unduly prejudiced against the speaker or what he has to say fail to learn it. That is why we may say that parables either clarify or cloud the message, depending upon how it is received. The clouding problem is not in the parable, but in the one who comes to it in the wrong way. Jesus explained this matter in Matthew 13 in response to the disciples' question about why He spoke to the crowd in parables (v. 10). He did so, He said, "because knowledge about the secrets of the kingdom from the heavens has been given to you, and it hasn't been given to them" (v. 10). But what did He mean by that? He further explained:

> *Whoever has will be given more, and he will have more than he needs,[1] but whoever doesn't have it, even what he does have will be taken away from him. This is the reason why I speak to them in parables, because though they see they don't see, and though they hear they don't hear, nor do they understand. Indeed, Isaiah's prophecy is fulfilled by them ... (He then quotes from Isaiah 6:10) "But your eyes are blessed, since they see; and your ears, since they hear." (Matthew 13:11-16).*

The fact that Jesus saw both possibilities in preaching through parables is interesting. Evidently, He did not believe in casting pearls to pigs (Matthew 7:6)! There is no doubt that in speaking to a mixed group in which some are hostile and others are friendly to the person or his message, a parable may have both effects. And on those occasions when one must speak before such a congregation of people, it would be doubly wise to consider delivering the message in parabolic form.

Another characteristic of some of Jesus' parables is exaggeration. The camel going through the eye of a needle, and swallowing a camel while straining out a gnat are examples.[2] In addition, it is hard to forget the slave who had been forgiven zillions and who goes out and tries to choke a few bucks out of another. In these parables, notice also the extremes that are contrasted.

---

1 This is a very important fact. We are never at a loss for help in the revelation that God has provided. It is more than enough!
2 Clearly, Jesus liked humor as well.

Parables, as we noted before, are taken from daily life—people in action or some aspect of animal and plant life. They are not fables and they are not allegorical. But they do, at times, use exaggeration, as we noted above. While a camel going through the eye of a needle is beyond possibility, it is something that is clearly understandable in terms of the elements concerned.

Parables usually call for decisions. They do not always do so overtly, but sometimes have an appendix or prologue that does so. At the conclusion of the parable of the Good Samaritan, Jesus says, "Go and do likewise."

The parables are in the past tense. They are told as one ordinarily tells a story.

Parables may be used during disputes with those who oppose the open preaching of the Word. In such cases, the parable may be designed to be understood by opponents and give force to the message (cf. Luke 20:19).

When of any length, parables usually include dialogue.

They were spoken in open-air settings where some of the elements of the parable may have been visible as Jesus spoke. In speaking about wheat and tares growing together, or the beauty of the lilies of the field, or even about a sower going forth to sow, He may have been able to point to an example near Him and His listeners.

These parabolic features, then, are elements and devices that the modern preacher must himself employ when composing parables if he would use them effectively. To understand what they are and how they are used will greatly facilitate parable-making. I advise you, then, to spend time studying the parables of Jesus. After all, one-third of the recorded speech of Jesus is in parabolic form!

Chapter Eight
Let's Begin

So far, we have taken time to examine various aspects of Jesus' use of the parable. Now, we shall make a preliminary start at composing a parable from a proverb. I have opened Proverbs at random (rather than select one that might be considered easier than the rest to use). The verse that my eye fell upon is Proverbs 14:4:

> *Where there are no cattle the stall is empty, but by the strength of an ox comes much increase.*

This fascinating and important verse is an excellent one to begin with. How do we do so?

First, we must understand what the proverb teaches. Its meaning is transparent: it is easier to keep the stall clean ("empty") when there is no animal present to foul it. But without the animal, there is no "increase" (profit). You can't have the one without the other. If you want to use the ox in order to earn a living, you must take care of him and his food and living quarters.

So far, so good. Having interpreted the verse (like most proverbs, that is easy to do),[1] we must ask "What is the principle embedded in the image (i.e., the generalization of which this particular application is one instance). That is also quite clear: added advantages increase responsibilities that, in turn, require time and effort.

But how shall we turn this principle into a parable? Think about the problem that it raises. Ask what it means in contemporary America. How many in our day fail because they want what the "ox" can provide without having to provide for the ox! A whole generation has grown up in which many expect to have what their parents have—and more—apart from the years of effort and struggle it cost their parents to obtain it. This verse is

---

[1] Which offers an additional reason for choosing proverbs as the basis for parables.

designed to awaken those who read to consider what is involved in an undertaking, purchase, or possession.

Well, that is clear enough. But how shall we turn it into a parable? By telling a story that inculcates this principle. There are a number of possibilities that may come to mind once you have the principle in hand. Here are a few of them:

- This could be used as a young people's talk. It might be turned into a parable of a young person who greatly wanted to buy an automobile. But, having saved and used all of his money to do so, then came the realization that with an automobile, one must have insurance, buy gas, pay for repairs, and so on. It might end up with the car in the garage, hardly ever used. Try your hand at developing this into the actual words of a parable.
- Another possible way of developing the proverb into a parable is to picture a person who wants to become an elder in a congregation, and only when he is elected to the position does he begin to realize what he has gotten into. The eldership is not all "sweetness and light." There are meetings to attend—sometimes long and tedious ones. There are counseling cases to become involved in (and, perhaps the need for training in this, which also takes time). There are hard decisions to make that other members of the congregation may not be too happy about. He may lose friends over those decisions, etc. Try once more to develop the principle into a full-blown parable.
- Or consider the following scenario. A young girl wants to be married. In time, her dreams are realized. But it isn't long before she recognizes that much of what she envisioned about married life was a dream! Now that she has fully awakened to the chores and problems of married life—keeping a home and a husband—she wonders whether she got into marriage precipitously. She may even be considering a divorce.

Now, how will your parables of the automobile owner, the elder, or the newly-married woman be presented? What do you intend to help the congregation see? Will you slant the parable toward avoiding carelessly jumping into obligations without considering the cost? Then your parables will be something like the parables of Jesus that had to do with deciding to build a tower before counting the cost, or the king who goes to war without considering the fallout.

On the other hand, you may pitch the parables toward urging those who have taken responsibilities upon themselves that they are not fulfilling. There is much profit (blessing) to be had in functioning well as an elder, for example. There are great rewards in marriage when one assumes her responsibilities. And the car owner who hastily purchased an automobile beyond his means may be urged to sell it and buy a less expensive one, or wait until he has money enough to care for it. In that scenario, the need for patience in assuming responsibilities may also be attached to the parable.

Certainly, from these few examples of parables that might be developed from one proverb, you can see many possibilities that lie in them. Notice that, in none of these thought starters was there any reference to oxen. So, there are two possibilities. You don't have to preach from the proverb as your text; you may simply use the proverb as a thought-starter for developing a parable that will help drive home the same point of another passage.

But I am sure that you have noticed that I have not yet fully developed these proverbs into parables. How would you go about it?

You would begin as I have by thinking of situations to which the general principle might be applied. Perhaps you may think of more than one and cannot decide which of the two or three you'd especially like to use. One possibility, then, is to do what Jesus did in Luke 15. He included three parabolic-like units into one, giving the last in the series a twist. In this way, you will be gaining assent ("Yes, that's what shepherds do"; "Yes, that's what women do"; "Yes, that's what fathers do") only to twist the final unit in a way that jars that harmony since it does not fit in parallel with the other units.

Or, perhaps, you don't want to use the three parables in succession. What will you do then? You have three parables that you think would equally do what you want to do in your sermon. How will you choose? Well, if they are all equally good, ask, "Which is most likely to ring bells with my congregation?" If you still can't distinguish them that way, ask, "Which can I develop most cogently using dialog, suspense, and so forth?" If these factors don't help you decide, and you conclude that any one of the parables would be as appropriate as any of the others in this sermon, toss a coin a couple of times and choose one. Then open your Parable Book[2] in which you will record the other two for future use!

---

[2] I strongly suggest that you keep such a book to preserve ideas either in fully-developed parable or in seed bed form. You will find it helpful in days to come.

Let's try one. Pass by the auto example and the elder problem, but when you come to the newly-married girl, stop. You may have her decide before the year is over that "marriage is not for me." She may then determine to get a divorce with all of its complications and heartaches (which you might describe). Then, you will determine how to warn the congregation of the outcome.

Now that we have walked through the preliminary steps of parable making from Proverbs, surely you see how simple it is to construct parables from the book of Proverbs. Let's turn next to the finishing touches necessary to shape the parable-to-be from a thought starter into its final parabolic form.

Chapter Nine
Shaping Up

In the last chapter I took the consideration of a proverb as far as getting the basic ideas for three parables (we might have developed many more). But I did not flesh these out so that they were fully developed. In this chapter, I plan to do just that. Let us take a different proverb this time. Having worked through the one in the last chapter, and after reading this chapter, you will be able to go back and give the finishing touches to the three possible parables that were only partially developed.

The proverb we shall now consider is as follows: "The naïve person believes every word, but the prudent man considers his step" (Proverbs 14:15). Again, there is nothing difficult about the exegesis of the verse; its meaning (as in many parables) is immediately apparent. The simple, unwise person, who doesn't know any better, will get into trouble because he believes everything he hears. He never checks out newspaper articles or the words of TV commentators to be sure that what they say is true. If a preacher says something from the pulpit, he believes it—whether or not there is good reason to do so. In short, he is gullible. If something is "religious," he thinks it must be right. He is a sucker for every advertisement that he encounters. He has no screens in the windows of his mind.

In contrast, the prudent (cautious, thoughtful, careful) man knows that the Bible teaches that this world of sin is filled with error, and that people are constantly pointing others to wrong ways. He is prudent, and therefore, he will not take a step forward in any direction that he has not fully considered and knows it is right. Unlike the naïve, he has screens at every window! Ultimately, he depends solely upon the Scriptures to guide him. Indeed, every thought or practice that he accepts, he filters through biblical screens. In this way, he keeps the "bugs" out!

Now, what sort of thought starters arise from the proverb? Many could, as I have already shown. I have intimated that the verse might refer to the problem of listening to the views of false teachers. There is much about false teaching in the Bible and how we ought to learn to avoid it. John severely warned Christians that they might lose their reward by careless acceptance of heresy (2 John 8). In a day when there is so much false teaching—even from supposedly "Bible-believing" churches—one cannot be careful enough.

The biblical passage upon which you will preach your sermon (and in which you plan to use the parable) might be Acts 17:11. In that passage, Luke says that the Berean Jews were more noble than those in Thessalonica because they "searched the Scriptures daily" to see whether what Paul and his companions taught was true. As a result, many believed. Clearly, to use the parable above would be appropriate—and probably memorable—if properly constructed.

Now, let's consider another scenario. Perhaps the congregation has not been giving enough money to the church. The Proverb may be quite appropriate as a text for a sermon dealing with this problem. Along with other exhortations, the preacher might mention the folly of sending checks to every cause his members hear about on TV or the radio, or in answer to the mail that comes across their desks. While many of these causes might be good ones, not all of them are. Consequently, in discussing prudence in giving, he might raise two matters: Have you investigated each organization carefully? Have you considered what, among the many good causes that appeal, should gain your *first* support? Some are swayed by emotionalism. They truly believe every crisis appeal demands their hearty response. Yet, how often do they stop to consider why the organization that is making the appeal didn't use more prudence and avoid such crises? Moreover, some fail to remember that when they became members of their local church they took vows to support that congregation (at least in our church people do). And, since one cannot give in answer to every appeal, and must choose those to which he donates, he must be sure that the church is not short-changed. In order to be prudent, members should consider which cause to put ahead of others. One who "considers" his ways will prudently conclude that his church should come before the rest. Rather than give what is left over to the church, it should be the other way around. After all, the preacher cannot carry on his ministry properly if he is paid a meager salary because his people are supporting other causes.

Take an additional scenario: one church member offers another the opportunity to "get in on a good deal." Because the brother making the offer seems to be a fine person who knows much Scripture, he thinks nothing could go wrong. No agreement is signed. Indeed, the deal is concluded with not even a handshake. He hands over a considerable amount of money—entirely on the word of the fellow member. The deal falls through; he loses his money, and there is no recourse. He ought to have investigated both the offer and the person making it. What is involved? Does the offer sound feasible? What is the financial track record of the brother he trusts? The prudent man looks well to his ways; he is not naïve. This, too, could be developed into a powerful parable.

But let's factor in one more item. The Proverb lauds prudence *over against* naivety. The contrast between these two lifestyles might suggest contrasting the ways of two people faced with a similar decision. One is naïve, the other prudent. It is this third option, as an extension of the first, that we shall shape into a parable (you can work on the other two at your leisure).

A naïve person is one who fails to give adequate thought to what others urge him to do. He runs headlong into trouble because he "believes every word." There is a place for doubt.[1] It is prudent for a man to "consider his steps." From a biblical perspective, of course, prudence is not pragmatic. The prudent person is always asking, "What would God have me do?"[2] The answer to that will be found in the Bible, and the Bible alone. The prudent person does not think first of himself, and the outcome of his actions, but of how to please God—whatever the outcome. Though many might not think so, the martyrs who gave up their lives rather than call Caesar "God" were prudent. So, prudence is not asking, "What would be to my immediate advantage?" It is considering the ultimate, eternal consequences of one's decisions. Prudence, then, requires careful consideration of how God's standard of faith and life applies to any given situation. Keeping this in mind, let's construct a parable.[3]

---

1 Not about God or His Word, but about what man may say.
2 Not WWJD ("What Would Jesus Do?"). This popular slogan allows a person to take whatever course of action he thinks Jesus would, but it does not base that action on biblical principles of conduct. And, remember, the God-man Jesus did many things we cannot or should not do.
3 Notice how we have thought through what the verse means in and of itself. Then, we looked at it in the larger context of the entire written revelation God has given. From this we developed a Scriptural understanding of prudence. From that point, we can

You are about to preach on Hebrews 5:11-14. Here is a pointed word about becoming dull of hearing from not training oneself to be able to distinguish good from evil—a serious problem in the church today. At the appropriate time in your sermon you might tell the following parable:

> Two men were invited to an evangelistic meeting. The evangelist preached with great oratorical power and persuasiveness. One man became quite enthused about what he heard. He bought several of the evangelist's books and tapes and put a large check in the offering plate when it was passed. The other man was cautious and wondered about some of the things the evangelist said. So he went home and studied his Bible to see whether what he heard was true. The first man continued to attend the evangelist's meetings, and after some days, he was baptized into the evangelist's church, which he now believed to be the only true church of Christ. The second man determined from Scripture that the evangelist's teaching that it was necessary to be baptized in order to be saved was wrong. He warned his friend, but being naïve, he refused to listen. The naïve man was caught up in falsehood, while the prudent man rejected it. I tell you that the second man rather than the first pleased his Lord.

Can you see the relevance of the Parable to the preaching portion in Hebrews? Is it not a warning against dullness of hearing and a call to prudent, biblical discernment?

Without saying that the heretical, so-called Church of Christ must be avoided, and not inferring that this is the only group that you are warning about, you have done several things at once. You have warned against naivety, counseled prudence, and applied this to the problem of accepting error because of enthusiasm. You have also pointed to the Bible as the source of truth. And you have done all of this (and more) in one parable.

While these matters are of importance and may be of help, we have not yet reached the point where we know when to use a parable, in what place in the sermon, and for what purposes. In the next chapter, we shall take a look at these things.

---

move ahead to flesh out a parable complete with its finishing touches.

Chapter Ten

When and Where to Use Parables

As we have seen, there are a number of factors that may shape the contours of a parable. But it is also true that the parable may shape the sermon. Indeed, a sermon may either be built around the parable in part or as a whole. Sometimes Jesus began with a question which led into the sermon.[1] In cases where a sermon begins with a parable, the rest of the sermon may actually grow out of it.

But when and where should parables be used in the sermon—that is an important matter to think about for a bit. I have already mentioned that a parable tends to make the listener think. If you want your congregation to ponder some significant thought, it might be wise to embed this truth into a parable: "What I have been saying is like …" Since the meaning of many of Jesus' parables was not immediately apparent, the disciples had to ask Him for an explanation. If they had thought about what He said, pondering it in their hearts, they might have both come to an understanding of His words and have had an opportunity to grow in their ability to understand and interpret His words. Hanging parables (ones to which the gospels give no explanation) are obviously intended to bring about this effect.

Parables may also make the truth one wishes to emphasize concrete. From the parable, people may see how to apply a principle to everyday life. In such cases it serves not only an interpretive purpose but also a demonstrable one. Often, people fail to see the practicality of an abstract teaching, but can grasp more readily what the teaching means in actual experience from a parable in which the truth is spelled out into concrete form. So, whenever the need for concreteness is present, consider using a parable to demonstrate how the truth "pans out" in daily life.

---

[1] Cf. Mark 3:23; 4:24ff.; Luke 14:7, 11; 12:41 In all of these instances, take note, the expected answer to the question is "No."

In addition, note how a parable may make a truth memorable. Congregations often have difficulty in remembering truth presented in the abstract—even when they comprehend it at the time when it was preached. If, however, one has ever heard the parable of the Good Samaritan or the parable of the Wheat and the Tares, he is not likely to forget it. All you need to do is repeat those identifying words to him and, immediately, the story with its message appears on his mental computer screen. If your parable is memorable, then it is one way to help members of the congregation recall what they would otherwise be likely to forget.

"OK, I can understand those things. But what about some help on when and where to place a parable in a sermon?" you ask. That is a good question. Of course, the when and the where converge. Either may call forth a concern about the other. Parables should occur in those places in sermons where they are needed.

One significant place for a parable is at its end, as a conclusion to the sermon. That is where Jesus placed the parable of the Two Foundations: it concluded His great Sermon on the Mount. Closing the sermon that way emphasized the need to do what He had been teaching—not merely to marvel at what they had heard. So, if you want to drive your message home, or call for action (as Jesus did), place a parable at the end of the sermon.

Other places to insert parables (and there may be more than one place in a sermon) are as follows:

- At the beginning, to arouse interest and lead the congregation into the message itself.
- When you need to show the practicality of your main point, if it is difficult to do so by simple exposition. You may want your listeners to recognize that you are not setting forth mere platitudes that are impractical. You want to show them that what you are saying may be done and that doing, or not doing it, may have significant consequences for them.
- At any place where you must clarify a difficult-to-understand matter. You can drop the parable into the sermon prior to the statement of the principle (in much the same way as you would in an introduction) or following the statement as an example or demonstration of it.[2]

---

2   With not quite as much emphasis as you would at the conclusion of a sermon.

These seem to be the principal factors to understand about the placement of parables. It is not necessary for every sermon to contain a parable. Perhaps there should be more that do than do not. But there is one warning to remember: parables are to be introduced into sermons only when they serve a greater purpose than mere variety. While they do lead to variety—breaking the cadence of the rest of the sermon—this is not a legitimate purpose for using them. They should always be used in a way that enhances the proclamation of God's truth.

It is not difficult, as you can see, to determine when a parable should be used and where it may be placed in a sermon, but just how does one go about doing so? How may he do so smoothly rather than in an awkward or disruptive manner? That is the subject of the next chapter.

Chapter Eleven
Placing the Parable

Having determined that a parable is needed, how will you go about introducing it into the sermon? Will you abruptly begin to tell the parable without warning, or will you somehow lead up to it? The answer is that you ought to do both—according to the purpose you have in including it.

You may send parables out of the blue like a bolt of lightening, only to have them disappear just as quickly. The listener hears the crack of thunder and, struck with your word, he is left hanging as to its meaning. Parables like these require one sort of approach; others, coming replete with introductions or conclusions must be placed differently. Each has its own purpose and, therefore, its own placement in the sermon. Since parables may be used almost anywhere in a sermon to meet a specific need, you must know precisely why you intend to use them. Then, alone, can you know just how to bring them into the sermon. These disparate purposes force you to vary the sort of parables that you use.

Often, in order to make a parable "stand out" from the rest of the sermon, you will want to pause—long enough to indicate that something especially important is about to be said. In such instances, at the conclusion of the parable, another pause may be appropriate. By pausing, you set the parable off from the rest of the sermon as you do in a paragraph in printed material to give prominence by means of leaving "white space" before and after it.

At other times, you may wish to prepare the listener for the coming parable as Jesus did when He said, "The kingdom of heaven is like ..." thereby indicating that He was about to make some sort of comparison, presumably to further explain what He had already said in straightforward exposition. Clearly, this sort of placement is designed to help by comparing the unknown to the known.

The third way in which you may introduce a parable into a sermon is shown by Jesus in Luke 15, the parable that we looked at in Chapter Four.

This three-part parable with a "kicker" at the end was juxtaposed to a previously mentioned circumstance (vv. 1, 2). A parable of this sort is used to solve a problem that has been mentioned, give an explanation to a question that had been posed, or (as in Luke 15) to condemn and call to repentance.

The introductory or concluding "hints" that I just mentioned must be clearly structured and made known in your preaching, or the listeners will find it difficult to interpret your parables. This is true, especially of those parables that are difficult to understand. It is also important, when you use them as transitions, to do so smoothly. Some of Jesus' parables were easy to understand. After relating the parable of the mustard seed, for instance, Mark tells us, "So with many such parables He spoke the Word[1] to them as they were able to hear" (Mark 4:33). The word "hear" in this passage means "understand." Plainly, this verse indicates that Jesus adapted His parables to His hearers' ability to receive them. And to be certain that His disciples *did* understand, He explained those parables to them (v. 34).

A certain University English teacher who was teaching composition in a writing class was rambling on about the difference between abstract and concrete language usage. Since his lecture consisted entirely of abstract principles and strategies, many students in his class failed to grasp much of what he said. Consequently, they learned little. What should that professor have done differently?

The answer, of course, is that at this stage in the book, I must do for you what he should have done. And that is exactly what I shall do in the next chapter.

---

1 N.B., a parable is not merely an illustration; it is a means by which God reveals truth.

Chapter Twelve
How To Do It

Let's consider the introductory or concluding use of a parable in a sermon. Let's say that you will be preaching from Hebrews 10:25,

> *We must not abandon our practice of meeting together as some are in the habit of doing.*

You want to exhort the congregation about this matter since there has been a certain laxness on the part of some. So, how do you go about it? Clearly, there are a number of ways, but here we shall look at one of them.

You are concerned to place emphasis upon the *foolishness* of "abandoning the practice of meeting together." In doing so, your thoughts naturally turn to the book of Proverbs because it so fully exposes foolishness and its consequences. After looking up "foolishness" in your concordance and not finding what you want, in flipping the pages of that book, your eye lights on Proverbs 18:1:

> *He who separates himself from others seeks to satisfy his own desires; he will roll headlong against sound wisdom.*

"Ah!" you say. "Perhaps this is what I want." So, you exegete the proverb and find that the word translated "roll" has in it the idea of propelling oneself (often violently) against something. Here, that something is "wisdom." It is clear that the one who does so is foolish. You have your verse. Now, you look at it more closely. And several facts emerge:
1. Solomon is describing a lone wolf, a recluse, or a self-sufficient person
2. Who doesn't think he needs others—and that would include other members of the church.

3. Why does he think that way? Because he is self-centered, wanting to spend his time and energies upon himself. He wants to satisfy his own desires and knows that if he becomes a part of the lives of others he cannot do this the way that he wants to.
4. Since he wants to assume no responsibility for the welfare of others, he becomes all wrapped up in himself,
5. And he rationalizes that he can study the Bible for himself; he doesn't need someone to preach to him. After all, doesn't the Bible speak of the priesthood of all believers?
6. Because he is all wrapped up in himself, he finds it desirable to "sleep in" on most Sunday mornings.

More might be said about this man, but this is sufficient. Now, you ask, "How about the result of such an attitude?" What are the results of such a self-sufficient attitude?

1. The verse indicates that this man doesn't think about the consequences of his actions—he rolls impetuously forward against sound wisdom. That is to say, he is a fool (in Proverbs, those who neglect God's wisdom are fools).
2. This unwise attitude by which he strongly butts up against God's wisdom, doubtless, stems from his personal pride in thinking that he is self-sufficient.
3. The consequence of opposing wisdom, implied in the second half of the verse, is that he will soon be brought up short. To forsake wisdom, Proverbs says again and again, is folly that leads to serious consequences—even to death (Proverbs 14:12).

Next, it is necessary to abstract from these many exegetical observations those elements that will serve most fittingly into a story that exposes the folly of "going it alone." Suppose we settle on these key concepts:

1. Separation from others
2. Seeking to satisfy one's own desires
3. Foolishly acting in a very unwise way
4. Serious consequences.

While other elements may be mentioned throughout the sermon, you decide to focus on these when building the story into a parable. You also decide that, rather than conclude the sermon with your parable, you will use it for an introduction. Here's the parable you composed:

There was a certain man who owned a business that was barely keeping afloat financially. One of his most trusted employees came and said to him, "I have a suggestion that might improve production and save money at the same time." But the owner was unwilling to listen, saying, "I don't need any suggestions from you; get back to work." Later, one of his sales reps came to him and urged him to adopt a policy that would boost sales. But he answered him the same way. The company continued to lose business, some of his finest workers took jobs elsewhere, and ultimately, the company failed.

Having introduced the sermon with this parable you might continue by asking, "Have you ever known anyone like that?" Indeed, you might even continue, "Do you find a tendency to try to live your life successfully apart from the advice and help of others? Well, let's consider a passage in which we read about Christians who attempted to do so, and were strongly reprimanded by God for it. In Hebrews 10:25 we read …"

You have launched the sermon. Following the parable, the sermon might proceed along lines following the outline below:

I. It is possible for you to fall into this foolish habit
II. If you foolishly focus on your own interests
III. To the neglect of others and their help

Of course, there are many other ways that you could go. Indeed, you have chosen only some of the factors that you might have. Others might be used in another sermon in the future. However, Proverbs 18:1 provides enough material to build a complete parable that enhances your message from Hebrews 10. I have not fleshed out the outline above because the making of sermons is not our present concern. For further help in that venue see my book, *Preaching With Purpose*.

In the next chapter, we shall consider how to drop a parable into the body of a sermon.

Chapter Thirteen
Internal Parables

We have looked at how parables may be used as the introduction or conclusion to a message, but have yet to consider using them internally. I have previously suggested that when you do, you leave "white space" around them. That is to say, make them stand out by pausing before and after them. This space before the parable gives the listener an indication that something different—perhaps of extra significance—is about to occur. And the pause following the parable allows time to think it through and apply it. That is one way to "drop" a parable into a sermon. I use the term "drop" because while the parable should be integrated into the rest of the message, it should also stand out as an entity in itself. In doing so, the listener will have something to take away with him (in the form of a story) by which to remember the thrust of the message.

Let's suppose that you are preaching on Matthew 6:33, "But seek first His kingdom and His righteousness, and all of these things will be added to you." While there are many ways in which you might preach a message from this verse, let's assume (for the sake of our example) that you will preach according to the following format:

Introduction
    I. You Are Seeking Something
        A. A part of your constitution to do so
        B. You may not know what it is
        C. It is time to find out
    II. You May Be Seeking What Unbelievers Seek
        A. Exposition of vv. 25-32
        B. These are temporal things
        C. Wrongly considered basics by Maslow, etc.
    III. You Should Seek God's Kingdom First
        A. To belong to it

      B. Then, to serve in it for eternal purposes (vv. 19-21)
      C. Here drop in your Parable
  IV. Make This A Matter of Priorities
      A. Seek these heavenly things FIRST
      B. And—as a by-product—God will provide for your basic needs.
  V. Conclusion

Now, I have never preached this passage before in this way. I am not even sure that I would do so were I to preach it again. But, for the sake of inserting a parable, take the outline or leave it. The outline is unimportant for our present concern.

Note, the parable comes near the end, but not at the end of the message. Placing it near the end makes it easier for the listener to take it away with him. It also sets up point four in the outline, which is the emphasis to carry away, namely, seeking God's kingdom and righteousness FIRST. That is to say, making this a priority.

Now, what sort of parable would fit in this place? Proverbs 24:27 provides just what we want:

> *Prepare your work outside and make it fit for yourself in the field, then, afterwards, build your house.*

This proverb, with its striking imagery, might be simply expanded so as to stress the principle embedded in it—put first things first. Here is one way in which you might do so:

> In homesteading days a young, ambitious farmer struck out to make a living on a fertile plot of ground on a western prairie. Immediately, he began building his house. He worked hard throughout the spring and late into summer, and by harvest time he was ready to move in. But when the harvest came, he had no crop to harvest. He had failed to put first things first!

At this point, it would also be appropriate to continue, saying, "He made the serious mistake mentioned in Proverbs 24:27 which reads …"

In the conclusion, you might warn about those who work (often very hard) throughout their lives for temporal things, but fail to sow the spiritual seeds that will bring in an abundant heavenly harvest (vv. 19-21). You will notice that in the conclusion, you will be alluding to the parable once more. That would nicely wrap up the sermon in a figure that grows out of the parable which the listener could carry with him as he leaves.

Chapter Fourteen
Parables and Illustrations

Parables are closely akin to the modern illustration. But there is a difference. The illustration seeks only to explicate, to demonstrate, and to concretize. In those respects, some parables are identical with illustrations. Parables, in distinction from illustrations, may also be used to cloud the truth from the minds of those who oppose it. Moreover, parables may leave the listener hanging, whereas an illustration has failed if it does so. Worded properly, the illustration is clear and obviously related to the truth that it illustrates. To fail in the matter of clarity is to fail to illustrate properly.

A parable may, as I have said, leave the listener without an explanation. The reason for this, we have seen, is to make the listener think. It is to give him something to chew on, to meditate on over a period of time. The illustration, if well composed, should immediately set forth the truth the preacher wishes to declare. The illustration, if it has been so vivid, may also have failed since it may capture the listener's attention so fully that he misses much else in the sermon. We have all heard people say things like "I don't know what he was illustrating, but the story was surely interesting," or "I can't remember the sermon, but I'll never forget the illustration." That is the opposite of what the parabolic preacher intends. While he is interested in the rest of the sermon and hopes that people will remember it, he is delighted if the parable stands out or calls attention to itself. That is one goal in using a parable. He wants the parable to be memorable in ways such that, if the listener remembers it, he will also remember the truth it presents. That is why the words "The Good Samaritan" are so powerful. They immediately bring back the story and, because the truth is so tightly bound up in it, the truth as well.

Now, there are parables that are closer to illustrations—especially those that either explain or have introductions or conclusions that give strong hints about what the parable teaches. Even here, however, there seems to be a difference. Without always saying it, the illustrator virtually says, "Now let me illustrate that. You see …" Good parables do not do that—either in so many words or in the way they are introduced. They always come as something of a surprise that demands special attention. Typically, they have a twist to them, shock the listener, or use hyperbole. While some of these elements may be found in an illustration, they are not as frequent, and may—if not used skillfully—so call attention to themselves that much of the rest of the sermon is forgotten. This is a cardinal sin in an illustration; it is a virtue in the parable.

So, while the parable and the illustration have much in common (they both may be stories, they are both analogous to some truth), there are striking differences. The parable is not to be thought of as primarily an example (as illustrations usually are), but is intended to have a more lasting quality; something the listener is able to carry away with him. The parable is so tied to the truth that the two cannot be separated. The parable is intended to exemplify the truth that it may dwarf all else in the sermon—not in an objectionable way, but for the sake of the truth.

If these things make sense to you, you will begin to understand something of the distinction between parable and illustration and will endeavor to construct parables along different lines than you are in the habit of doing when seeking or creating illustrations. The parable requires skill in determining how to so state the truth by a story, or other means, that it is *not* a mere illustration—but something more, something greater. In that sense, it may be said to be an illustration *par excellence*.

Take care, then, when developing and placing parables that you do not confuse them with illustrations. Otherwise, they will lack the distinctive character that they must possess in order to achieve the ends just mentioned.

Chapter Fifteen
Practice in Expanding Proverbs

Now is the time for you to begin putting the things that you have learned into practice. In this chapter, I shall choose some verses from Proverbs that readily lend themselves to expansion into parables. I shall get you started on each, but will stop short of composing the parable. That is where you will take over.

Notice in the heading of this chapter, I have indicated that your task will be to *expand* proverbs into parables. In the next chapter, you will *extract* a principle from a Proverb and *extend* it to other scenarios. This two-fold use of proverbs should be clearly understood. When expanding a proverb, the scenario that is presented by the proverb is basically left undisturbed. Rather than change the scenario, the task is to expand it. In expanding the proverb, it is viewed as a mini-parable that may be expanded into a full-blown parable.

On the other hand, in the process of extending a proverb, the principle embedded in the proverb is extracted and then applied (or extended) to other scenarios. The process that I am here calling extension, earlier I referred to as generalizing.

In using Proverbs as a source for your parables, you should always determine whether you will expand the proverb or extend the principle embedded in it. In either case, it is important to understand the principle (or truth) since it is that which will become the point of your parable.

So, let's begin.

1. **Proverbs 13:11:** *Wealth that comes from nothing will dwindle, But he who gathers by the work of his hand will increase it.*

Here you have a proverb that lends itself to expansion. Its meaning is fairly plain. A person who gains wealth some other way than by working for it finds that it dwindles. That is to say, if he depends on it, rather than working to increase it, it will do so. In contrast, the one who has worked hard ("gathered by the work of his hand") will increase his wealth. Large inheritances, for instance, frequently dwindle over the succeeding generations. Money obtained from gambling, theft, and other nefarious undertakings usually dwindles even more rapidly. But the one who "gathers" wealth through his industry will increase that wealth rather than chip away at it.

There you have it. Now, try your hand at creating a story that fits the scenario described in this proverb.

2. **Proverbs 14:1:** *A wise woman builds her house, but a foolish one pulls it down with her own hands.*

There are foolish women who, today, destroy their marriages and families. It seems strange that they would work hard at doing so rather than expend their efforts to build them up. Sometimes, by their actions, they "pull down" in later years everything they have spent their earlier years building up. Foolish habits of overspending, resentment, rebellion against biblical principles, and unwillingness to discipline children are among the possibilities that you may explore in finding the very best way to develop the scenario. Have a go at it!

3. **Proverbs 14:9:** *Stupid fools mock at guilt, but among the righteous is favor.*

People who think that they can make light of their sin are foolish. The mocking might take the form of denial that what he said or did was sin ("Oh come on now, I was just having fun") or it may be a scornful attack upon biblical morality ("What you call sin is no more than a predisposition that no one can help; we are born with different temperaments and genetic make-ups. Get a life!"). He is interested, perhaps, in removing or lessening his guilt. Here is a proverb that in this day should ring bells for you!

4. **Proverbs 15:1:** *A soft answer turns away wrath, but a foolish word stirs up anger.*

The verse needs no further explanation. When attacked by another, how one responds usually determines what will happen in the end. That response will either calm the situation or inflame it. Certainly, this proverb may be expanded to a number of parabolic scenarios, such as those verbal conflicts that occur at work, in the home, or between church members.

5. **Proverbs 15:19:** *The way of a lazy person is like a road blocked by thorns, but the path of a righteous person is built up.*

A little exposition is necessary here. The lazy person has allowed weeds and thistles to grow up along the pathway leading to his house (sometimes these paths might be rather long). Later, perhaps in a hurry to get somewhere, he finds his way blocked by thorns and thistles, thereby making progress difficult. He has not thought ahead—or if he has, he has neglected keeping his property well trimmed. After all, that requires work! The righteous person's pathway, in contrast, is not only thorn and thistle free, it is "built up." That is to say, it is a well-maintained passageway. Paths were built up so as to shed water, etc. This took work to maintain in the face of erosion and frequent use. The lazy person's neglect comes back to plague him, whereas the righteous man's work serves to help him later on.

How well did you do? If you wish, you may write these parables in your Parable Book mentioned earlier, thus making a good beginning at developing it. When you complete the next chapter's practice work, you will have ten parables to record in it. Since Proverbs may be either expanded or extended, you may want to divide your Parable Book into two sections corresponding to these two methods of developing parables from Proverbs.

Chapter Sixteen
Practice in Extending Proverbs

In developing a parable, a proverb may be *extended* as well as *expanded*. That is to say that the principle embedded in the proverb may be *extracted* and generalized (or, as I have called the process, "extended") to other situations. Extending is possible because a principle (or truth) is larger than any specific instance to which it is applied. The proverbs we shall consider will be of two types: those that are pictures or specific examples of the application of the principle, and those that are more-or-less statements of the principle. I say "more-or-less" because they are not precisely set forth in principle form (in ways that we might today).

As in the previous chapter, here I shall give a simple exposition of the proverb (including the principle extracted from it), followed by space for you to write in the parable (or parables) that you compose. I suggest that since you are extending the principle, you may find that more than one scenario will develop. The three-part parable of Luke 15, for instance, is so constructed that three examples (or mini-parables) of how the principle that Jesus is teaching applies to life are brought together to form a single one. While you may not want to construct a multi-faceted parable, you can see from the way that Jesus did it that one principle runs through the three parts:

1. Shepherds search for lost sheep and rejoice when found
2. Women search for lost coins and rejoice when found
3. Fathers look for lost sons and rejoice when found

The obvious principle (or truth) is that it is right to search for that which is lost and to rejoice when it is found. The Pharisees, like the elder brother, violated that principle by complaining rather than rejoicing with the angels in heaven when a lost sinner is sought and found. Actually, Jesus might have set forth the last scenario alone—that of the father and his son. But it was more powerful to demonstrate how far out of reality the religious leaders were by using three scenarios.

Well, let's get to the practice.
1. **Proverbs 15:21:** *Foolishness is a joy to the one who lacks sense, but a discerning man walks straight.*

What does this proverb mean? There are fools who lack sense (Literally, "lack heart," a Hebrew idiom for want of good sense). That is one of the reasons they act foolishly. Their lack of good sense is disclosed by the fact that they take pleasure in foolish ways. Unlike the discerning man, who will never get lost, but will remain on the straight path, the fool strays from the right path.

The principle is that those who delight in foolishness, whether it be ribald talk, hurtful acts, or other sinful activities, will walk crookedly in the paths of unrighteousness. A man who delights in mercilessly teasing a child or finds hurting an animal fun, will go astray in other, even more sinful ways. OK. Now you are in a position to develop a parable.

2. **Proverbs 15:32:** *He who refuses discipline despises himself, but he who hears reproof gets sense.*

Without realizing what he is doing, the one who refuses to learn from rebukes of discipline harms himself because he becomes more engrossed in sin. As a result, he loses opportunities to learn from wise persons who might help him (as v. 31 indicates). In contrast, the one who learns from ("hears") reproof grows in knowledge and prudence ("sense"). The principle is what? Figure it out for yourself and let your parable emerge from it.

3. **Proverbs 16:26:** *A worker's appetite works for him since his mouth urges him on.*

Here, the word "mouth" represents not speech (as it usually does), but hunger (for something to put in the mouth). A man will work for something to eat, if for no other reason. The need to provide for himself and for his family ought to spur him to get to work (cf. 2 Thessalonians 3:10). Again, what is the principle? Remember, though you may use a scenario inferred in the proverb, the principle is larger than that to which it is applied. What is it? State it in one succinct sentence (Forcing yourself to do so is always a good way to be certain that you understand it). How will you use it to form a parable exemplifying it?

4. **Proverbs 18:5:** *To be partial to the wicked isn't good; or to thrust aside the righteous in judgment.*

This proverb may refer to justice in the courts or to how an individual acts. Whichever way you may use it to form a parable, you should see that the proverb speaks about a reversal of God's revealed order. One reason for the high crime rate in our land is liberal judges who seem to take delight in letting the wicked off lightly. But this could be true of fearful elders or deacons who pander to people in their congregation who act sinfully and carry a big stick. In decision-making they are often placated while upright members are excoriated instead. I have given you strong hints here. Again, state the principle or truth in one concise sentence, and then embed it in a parable.

5. **Proverbs 18:13:** *He who answers a matter before he hears does a stupid and disgraceful thing.*

One should never jump to conclusions until he has all the pertinent facts. Otherwise, he makes it clear that he is a fool who deserves to be disgraced—even if that doesn't happen eventually when all of the facts come in. Having sufficient data before rushing to judgment is prudent and a characteristic of a wise man. Again, what is the principle? How will you develop a story that will set it forth?

Well, if you have worked hard at the practice sessions that I have provided for you in this chapter and the last, as I said before, you will now have a minimum of ten parables for your Parable Book. In addition, I suggest that you take the time each week to compose at least four parables from the book of Proverbs. In a short time, you will have a collection (which you might classify according to subject matter) upon which you will be able to draw when preparing sermons. Divide them (as suggested in the last chapter) into two basic divisions: 1) Expanded Proverbs; 2) Extended Proverbs. In that way, you can choose for variety and for the type of parable that most aptly achieves your purposes.

Moreover, I suggest that you continue to work through the book of Proverbs, beginning with Chapter Ten, until you have exhausted all of the possibilities. "Won't that limit the range of my parables?" No, because Proverbs contains so many principle truths that once you really get into the wealth of material found there, you will find it hard to exhaust the number of diverse truths that you discover. "But won't my people get tired of hearing me talk about parables?" No, because you will rarely be doing that. Rather, in Proverbs, you will find thought-starters that, once they take parabolic form, will not necessarily expose the source of your parables (not that it is wrong to do so at times). Once you begin to catch on to creating extended parables, you will rarely depend on the particular proverb from which you extracted the principle that you find yourself using.

So, best wishes as you practice. Don't give up. Remember, the Lord Jesus turned the land of Palestine upside down largely through the preaching of parables. And, of course, throughout the centuries, Christians everywhere have benefited from them. I suspect that as you begin to drop them into your sermons (especially those at hand), people will remark about your preaching and remember what you had to say.

Conclusion

THERE you have it! Reasons why parables should be used in preaching, an explanation of their place and usage, and a method for producing them. I hope you have found the book worthwhile. It is an instruction book, not an inspirational one. That's clear. But, if you have been tracking with me over the pages that precede, I think that you will have found inspiration in the very idea of making and using parables in preaching.

It was exciting to write this book. I do not think that it is definitive. Certainly not. But I do believe that anyone who takes the time and makes the effort to follow what he finds in it will be on a fast track toward preaching with parables. The method that I have set forth is simple. If you use the book of Proverbs as the basic source for learning to develop and use parables, you will have solved one of the principal problems that you might have otherwise encountered. Moreover, if you have followed the explanations and practiced the method set forth, in a very short time you will be able to regularly add parables to your sermons with striking force and power.

It will not be long before you will possibly learn to use a lengthy parable instead of a talk on special occasions such as a men's or women's meeting, a pastor's fellowship group, a youth outing, and so on. The methodology required is no different; the major adjustment to be made is to learn how to enlarge a parable to meet the situation. I do not advise that you use a lengthy parable as a substitute for a Sunday sermon. But in a Church School or Prayer meeting hour, it might be appropriate to do so from time to time.

At any rate, I trust that you will agree that if the concept is new to you, this book may have opened new vistas for your future preaching. It would be interesting to receive feedback about ways in which parables have enlivened your preaching.

Thank you for studying this book with me. I believe that you will want to tell your fellow pastors about the insights you have discovered and encourage them to attempt preaching parables as well.

Preaching to the Heart

Introduction

For years homileticians have been exhorting preachers to "preach to the heart." But what are they talking about? Do you know? Do *they?* Is the concept biblical, and if so, how does one do it? These and similar questions often remain unanswered, and the typical preacher goes on doing what he always has done, resigned to the assumption that says, "I'll never be a great preacher; I guess I'll never be able to preach to the heart."

Is that true? Does the capacity for preaching to the heart belong only to the exceptionally gifted? Or is it rather that preaching to the heart is a developed skill that makes preachers great? The whole concept has been presented in such a vague and fuzzy way that anyone unfamiliar with it would find it difficult or impossible to obey the injunction.

The blame for confusion about what it means to "preach to the heart" does not lie solely with homileticians, while preachers go off scot-free. Homileticians should make themselves clear. But if they don't, it is the responsibility of the preachers to pound on their doors until they do. So neither is guiltless. There has been a conspiracy of ignorance in which words and phrases have been uttered again and again as though the speakers and the listeners knew perfectly well what they were talking about, when all the while they did not. As a homiletician who has been at fault in this matter, I believe something must be done. It is time for the whole matter to be cleared up. That is the point of this book.

My purpose is to show that preaching to the heart is biblical and therefore necessary, and that any man with the gifts and heart for preaching can be taught clearly how to do it. Indeed, I propose to go even further: in the pages that follow I shall endeavor to teach him how to do so.

The first Christian sermon, preached on the day of Pentecost by the apostle Peter, was preached to the heart. Luke wrote:

> *Now when they heard this, they were stung[1] to the heart and said to Peter and the rest of the apostles, "Brothers, what should we do?" (Acts 2:37).*

That crowd response was the fruit of effective preaching, empowered by the Holy Spirit. But effective, heart-penetrating preaching can also lead to the opposite response:

> *Now when they heard these things, they were pierced through[2] to their hearts and gnashed their teeth at him (Acts 7:54).*

When Peter preached, great numbers repented and believed the gospel; when Stephen preached, his listeners killed him. Yet both were filled with the Spirit and preached to the heart. This double and opposite response makes one thing clear at the outset: while preaching to the heart is a desirable effect brought about by the power of the Spirit, the exact nature of that effect on the listener may vary greatly and cannot be predicted beforehand.

In either case, Spirit-empowered, biblical preaching strikes squarely at the heart. It elicits a response. No hearer can remain apathetic: *he must respond.* To speak of preaching to the heart, then, is to speak of preaching that brings a definitive response; it is preaching that evokes words and action from the listener.

Think of it—preaching that calls forth action! Preaching that gets results! Preaching that so stirs the listener that he must respond! That is what we need today.

Is there any reader who wouldn't like to preach or hear preaching like that? Is there any reader who *has* heard much preaching like that? Something is wrong; what has happened to our preaching? Why is that sort of preaching virtually unknown? That too we must investigate and decide what God wants us to do about it.

---

1 The verb, *katanusso*, is a strong term that means "to prick, to stun, to smite, to sting." This compound word is a combination of *nusso*, "to pierce, to puncture," and *kata*, a prepositional prefix that intensifies the action. The passive of the verb connotes being pricked or stung to the heart.
2 The verb *diaprio*, here translated "pierced through," is also used in Acts 5:33. It has in it the idea of "sawing through" (*prio* = "to saw, sever, bite," and *dia* = "through") and often carries the meaning of "cutting (through) to the heart."

Chapter One
What Is the Heart?

A clear idea of what the Bible means by *heart* is foundational to all else that we shall consider in this little book. Indeed, the widespread careless use of that word is responsible for the confusion and vagueness that surround exhortations to preach to the heart.

"But," you object, "everyone knows what *heart* means. I don't see why you are making such a fuss over it. Surely it doesn't take an entire chapter to define something so obvious, does it?" Yes. You see, that's exactly what is wrong: everyone thinks he understands the term, but very few do. Ask yourself, "Exactly what does the word *heart* mean in the *Scriptures?*" Can you give a precise definition? "Well, maybe not an exact one, but I know what it means, nevertheless."

Do you?

Let's test your understanding a bit, okay? What do you think of the often quoted sentiment, "What we need is more heart knowledge and not just head knowledge"? Do you think it does or does not convey an acceptable idea of *heart* as the word is used in the Bible?

"Well, I guess so, but I'm not sure; anyhow, I know what the sentence is getting at."

What?

"It is saying that it isn't enough to merely know truth, that truth must grip you—it has to affect your emotions as well."

You are probably correct about the way that sentence is used, but the fact is, it suggests an incorrect interpretation of the biblical word *heart*. If *heart* is used to refer to feelings or emotions as over against thought or intellect, that use is discordant with Scripture. Never in the Bible is the word *heart* set over against the head or the intellectual processes. That is a modern, Western idea of the heart, introduced into the Bible from the outside. One would never get that idea from the Bible itself. Indeed, that is a Roman rather than a biblical view of the heart. The Valentine's Day cupid, shooting arrows through little red or pink hearts, is the culprit behind this modern, unbiblical view. To Western origins may be attributed all of our romantic notions, which include the idea of heart-as-feeling. No such conception can be found in the Scriptures.

Consider instead what *is* contrasted with the word *heart* in the Bible. In Matthew 15:8, for instance, we read that the people honor God "with their lips, but their heart is far from" Him. That sort of contrast is regularly made in the Scriptures. You find the same thing in the well-known passage in Romans 10 in which we are told that it is not enough to confess Christ with the mouth; the one making the profession also must believe in his heart. Notice the contrast: heart/lips, heart/mouth. In the important passage 1 Samuel 16:7 we are assured that "man looks on the outward appearances but [in contrast] God looks on the heart." Plainly, in all of these pivotal passages, there is a contrast between the heart as something inner and the lips, mouth, and appearance as something outer. That is the true biblical contrast, not a contrast between intellect and emotion.

But what is this inner and outer man? The inner is called the "hidden person of the heart" in 1 Peter 3:4. The inner person is the one that the Lord alone knows—he is hidden from us; we look only at the outer man. That is one major reason why we must never judge a man's motives: we simply don't know what they are. Rather, we must judge only his actions and his words (i.e., those factors that *are* accessible to us).

The outer man is the manifest person, the one we are familiar with; the inner man is the person known only to God and, in part, to himself. This inner man is not his feelings. In the Bible, the notion of feelings is expressed by the word for viscera; we read, for instance, of "bowels of compassion." Clearly, the heart includes the whole inner man—the intellect along with the emotions as well. In the 14th Psalm there is a good example of the intellectual use where we are told that "The fool says in his heart that there is no God" (Ps. 14:1). Incidentally, he is a fool because he listens to one![1] Here we see the fool involved in an intellectual process: talking himself into a false belief. And so it goes throughout the Bible. In various passages,

---

[1] The fool, *nabal*, is not only one who is stupid, but one who is wicked and boorish. The Hebrew word refers to a falling leaf or a withered fruit. It has the notion of something useless, bad, abandoned and full of weakness and decay.

people are said to reason, plan, understand, think, doubt, perceive, make mistakes, purpose, intend, and the like in their hearts! One of the ways to say that a person lacks good sense is to say (translating literally) that he "lacks heart" (cf. Prov. 9:4, 16). Clearly, then, in the Bible, the word heart does not mean emotion.

With that false interpretation out of the way, we are prepared to ask what the word *heart* does mean as it refers to the inner man. It has several ideas folded together. *Heart* means good sense, as we have just seen, but it also means conscience (cf. Heb. 10:22; 1 John 3:9-21). It is the "treasure house" (Luke 6:45) from which one's actions and words flow. Putting these and other concepts of *heart* together we come to the conclusion that the heart is the inner life one lives before God and himself.[2] It is the source of the outer life (Matt. 15:19), and it expresses more certainly what a person is really like than what he does or says externally. That is why God "tries the heart." Thus, to do something "from the heart" is to do it genuinely. And to do it "with all your heart" is to do it wholeheartedly rather than with a "double" or divided heart.

A hypocrite is one who focuses on being "seen of men" rather than being seen by God; he pretends by his outward show of holiness to be something that, inwardly, he is not. It is possible to sin in the heart without committing any outward offense (Matt. 5:28). Only one person in the history of the world ever had both heart and outer appearance completely in sync at all times—Jesus Christ. The rest of us, as sinners, have various inconsistencies between the inner and outer life.

The word *heart* has become a devalued currency in our culture. Preachers too often read the modern Western view of heart-as-emotional-commitment back into Scripture and thus mistake and distort what the Holy Spirit moved the writers of the Bible to say. It is time to restore the true biblical content of the word so that we may profit from an understanding of those many passages in which it occurs.

If the heart of man in the Bible refers to the inner life, from which all else flows, what is the point of preaching to the heart? In light of this meaning, we may say that preaching that goes to the heart genuinely affects the person. He has been hit at the very source of his whole life (Prov. 4:23). He has been

---

2   For a fuller discussion of the word, see my book, *Theology of Counseling, More than Redemption*.

pierced by the preached Word where it counts. This does not necessarily mean that he is converted or, in the case of a believer, that he will repent of his sin, but it does mean that the sermon has truly hit home. That is why, whether the response is favorable or unfavorable, preaching that pierces the heart is preaching that elicits a response. It could not do otherwise because, as we have just seen, the heart is the source of every response. It also may be said that preaching that penetrates or cuts through to the heart is preaching that elicits a *genuine* response—whether it be faith or fury. Preaching that gets through to the heart does not leave the listener apathetic.

In contrast, preaching that does not go to the heart of a man is preaching without any genuine effect. While the listener may express gratitude for the help he has received, the words on his lips do not flow from heartfelt conviction. In time, his speech and actions will reflect the true condition of his heart. "By their fruits shall you know them." When the inner man is truly affected by the Word for good, that will lead to a positive, lasting change in his outward behavior. The outer and inner man will come into closer sync through discernible patterns of growth.

So, you can see how desirable it is to preach to the heart. Indeed, a strong biblical case could be made that unless preaching penetrates deeply enough to affect the inner life, it is not preaching at all. True biblical preaching changes people. It did in Bible times, and there is no reason why it will not do so today. We possess the same Spirit and the same Word by which and from which they preached. The only difference is that they preached to the heart and we so often do not. We must discover the causes of this failure in present-day preaching and apply the biblical cure.

Chapter Two
Two Kinds of Hearts

When the Word of God is preached, it receives two kinds of responses: some hearts are "hardened," and others are transformed. What is the reason for this difference, and what does it mean to the preacher of the Word?

First, note that these two responses are everywhere distinguished in the Bible itself. In the two verses from Acts mentioned in the introduction, we see the two responses in the plainest contrast. Although both Peter and Stephen preached in the power of the Holy Spirit, and the words of both penetrated their listeners' hearts, the responses to their preaching were exactly opposite: Peter's preaching resulted in many conversions, while Stephen's preaching infuriated his listeners, at the cost of his life. Luke's description of Stephen as a "man full of the Holy Spirit and faith" (Acts 6:5; see also 6:3, 10, 15, as well as 7:55, 56) makes it clear that neither his attitude nor his preaching was to blame for the negative response.[1] While preaching to the heart invariably gets results—either hot or cold, never lukewarm—there's no telling beforehand what the result will be.

Let's take a closer look at Acts 2:37 and 7:54, which I quoted in full in the introduction. In Acts 2:37, the crowd was "stung to the heart" by Peter's Pentecostal sermon, and in Acts 7:54, the result of Stephen's preaching was that members of the Sanhedrin were "pierced through to their hearts." Moreover, both sermons elicited action from those who heard: in the first instance, the listeners asked, "What shall we do?"; in the second, they "gnashed their teeth" and picked up stones to kill Stephen.

As I have pointed out, the difference in results stemmed not from the preachers themselves, or the types of sermons they preached, or the

---

[1] Stifler, in his all-but-forgotten, yet extremely valuable, book, *Introduction to the Study of the Acts of the Apostles*, makes a strong case for the direct inspiration of these early sermons in Acts. Whether he is correct or not, they do set before us a valuable pattern for preaching. But, how much more so if he is right (the idea here is that they were the fulfillment of Luke 21:12-15).

manner in which they preached; both preached under the full approval and power of the Holy Spirit, who expressly played a prominent part in both events. No, only one factor can account for the difference—the hearts of those who heard the Word.

Both groups heard the Word. Both took it to heart. In the first instance, Peter's message is said to have "stung" the heart. The word translated "stung" is *katanusso*, a Greek term that may also be translated "to strike or prick violently, to stun or to smite." Clearly, the word speaks of a strong impact or powerful jolt on the inner life. In the second instance, a different word is employed to describe the effect of Stephen's preaching on the Pharisees. It is *diaprio*, a word meaning "to saw asunder, or cut through to" as well as "pierce through." Again, this very forceful word describes an act in which all barriers to hearing have been penetrated. In both Peter's preaching and Stephen's, the heart was reached. But only in the first instance was the heart changed. Though in the second, the heart was strongly affected, it remained unchanged and responded negatively to the Word. So while preaching to the heart always *reaches the heart*—the inner man—and has an impact on it, one heart receives God's Word and is altered by it for good, whereas another hears it, rejects it, and turns on the one who preaches.

The Bible affirms throughout that there are two different sorts of hearts. In Ezekiel 36:16 we read about a "heart of stone" and a "heart of flesh." Peter's message was received by the latter, Stephen's by the former. The heart of flesh is warm and living, responsive to God's Word, while the heart of stone is dead and unresponsive. The difference is seen again and again. For instance, in Hebrews 6, a passage that some have found troublesome because it talks about professed Christians falling away (v. 6), the answer to the supposed problem is that, in time, those who have a heart of stone will manifest the fact as, indeed, those with hearts of flesh will; the first will fall away and the second will not. The passage does not teach that those who have good hearts will fall away, but only those whose hearts are stony. That is clear from verses 7–9, in which the two diverse sorts of hearts are referred to under the figure of two types of ground. Both receive the same rain—i.e., both have had the very same influences, including the preaching of the Word (cf. v. 6)—but the results in each type of ground are different. The one ground brings forth fruit, the other weeds. Clearly, the different responses to heavenly influences are due not to any difference in preaching (the rain is the same) but to differences in the hearts of the ones who hear it. In one case the Word is mixed with faith, while in the other it is not (cf. Heb. 4:2). So, the reason why the response to Peter's sermon was faith and the response to Stephen's was fury is that God's rain fell on two distinct types of ground.

There are many other examples in Scripture. Paul, for instance, has a lot to say about distinct types of hearts in 1 Corinthians 2. In verse 14 he asserts, "But a natural person doesn't welcome the teachings of God's Spirit; they are foolishness to him, and he isn't able to know about them because they must be investigated spiritually." Here, the person with the stony heart is called a "natural person." He is the person to whom nothing *super*natural has ever happened. He came into this world "dead in trespasses and sins," with a nature that is both corrupt and guilty before God, and nothing since has changed that picture. The natural person is in darkness because he has inherited a nature from Adam that is dead toward God and the teachings of His Spirit. He has no heart for God or the things of God. The spiritual person, also mentioned in this passage, is the person who has a heart of flesh. Something supernatural has happened to him: his old heart has been replaced and the Spirit of God now dwells in his inner life, enabling him to understand and otherwise respond positively to God's Word as it is preached.

The room in which you sit is full of sights and sounds, many of which you selectively block out of your mind. In the same way, the natural person, while surrounded by a vast display of God's glory, covers his eyes and ears to the many evidences for God's goodness. Indeed, he may show hostility whenever they are mentioned to him (especially if they are driven home to his heart). Paul puts it this way: "What eye hasn't seen and the ear hasn't heard, and what hasn't been conceived by the human heart is what God has prepared for those who love Him" (v. 9). The "human heart" is the heart as it is in its natural, unregenerate state. It is, as Isaiah said, a heart that has "grown thick," one that cannot "understand" (Acts 28:27), the heart over which a veil lies (2 Cor. 3:15); it will not respond favorably to God's Word until its "blindness" has been removed, so that the light of God's truth about Christ may shine in (2 Cor. 4:4–6).

Paul has made it plain that the things of God are prepared for and "*given*" (1 Cor. 2:10) to "those who love Him." But the natural, stony heart has no love for God. That love must be "poured into our hearts through the

Holy Spirit" as He is "given" (Rom. 5:5). Indeed, as Paul elsewhere asserts, "nobody can say, 'Jesus is Lord,' except by the Holy Spirit" (1 Cor. 12:3). It is in the giving of the Spirit that the new heart is given.

Since preaching to the heart is a matter of preaching to two different sorts of hearts, that distinction must be understood. Not that we must know *which* kind of heart we face. When Peter and Stephen preached, neither knew which kind of heart he was preaching to. God does not give us the right or the ability to look into other men's hearts; He reserves that privilege for Himself. Our task is to preach the Word effectively, so that it penetrates to the hearts of men; God opens the hearts to the preached Word as He sovereignly determines. Hearts are closed to God's truth until He opens them. Of Lydia it is written that "the Lord opened her heart to pay attention to what Paul said" (Acts 16:14). It is He who gives the "new heart" of "flesh" and removes the "heart of stone" (Ezek. 36:26). Again, according to this passage in Ezekiel, that happens only when God puts His Spirit in a man. Regeneration is God's work; the preacher regenerates no one. God Himself must "quicken," or give life to, those who are "dead in trespasses and sins" (Eph. 2). That life, that new heart, enables one to understand and believe the message when it reaches the heart. The heart is the soil upon which the seed is sown; if it is good soil, it will bring forth fruit; if not, there will be no harvest.

Chapter Three
Preaching from the Heart

How does one preach to the heart? In several chapters, I shall consider that question biblically. But any answer must begin with the observation that to preach to the heart, one must preach *from the heart*.

What do I mean by that? Simply this: a preacher of God's Word must be genuine. His inner belief and desire must correspond to the words he speaks. Another way to say the same thing is to say that he must be filled with the Holy Spirit. The Holy Spirit fills those who are genuine and gives them power to preach effectively. The powerful impact of the sermons of Peter and Stephen[1] can be accounted for in no other way than to say that the Holy Spirit was at work as they preached.

Consider what Luke wrote about Stephen: "But they couldn't stand up against the wisdom and the Spirit with which he spoke" (Acts 6:10). Calvin, commenting on this passage, says: "They could not resist the wisdom which the Spirit of God gave him.... the enemies of the gospel were therefore discouraged and overcome, because they did strive against the Spirit of God, which spake by the mouth of Stephen. And forasmuch as Christ hath promised the same Spirit to all his servants, let us only defend the truth faithfully, and let us crave a mouth and wisdom of him, and we shall be sufficiently furnished to speak...." Stephen was a man in whom the Spirit was at work; such men preach to the heart, because they preach from the heart. That heart is a heart dominated by the Spirit.

What does it mean to be *filled with the Spirit?* In that phrase, the idea of domination is uppermost. When the Bible speaks of being filled with amazement, with fear, with jealousy, or with joy, similarly, the idea of domination is in view. A person who is filled with fear is dominated by

---

1 Stephen's sermon must not be considered a failure because of the results. The failure was on the part of his listeners. Not only was it a success in God's sight because it exposed their sin, but it became the occasion for a persecution that pushed the gospel out of Palestine, where it had been bottled up, toward the ends of the earth.

fear; everything he does or says in that condition is colored by fear. His voice, his actions, his decisions, everything is under the influence of this dominant emotion. The same is true of one who is "filled" with jealousy, joy, or amazement.[2]

The important passage in which we are *commanded* to be filled with the Spirit (Eph. 5:18) sets up an informative contrast between the Spirit and wine. Wine dominates the drunkard so that all he does is under its influence; similarly, Paul says, the Holy Spirit's influence must dominate the whole of one's life.

How does the Spirit fill, dominate, or exert such total influence? Don't think of the Spirit's filling in terms of pumping gasoline into your automobile tank. Rather, the image of the church auditorium better fits the situation. When the church is "filled," every seat is taken. When a drunkard is filled with wine, every part of his life is affected by it; every area is under the influence of wine. It destroys his home life, his social life, his physical life, and his business life. That is why Paul wrote, "Do not be drunk with wine *which leads to utter ruin*" (the word for utter ruin is *asotia*, "unsavableness, beyond salvaging"). Paul warns of utter ruin, because there is nothing that escapes wine's influence; wine destroys *all* of the drunkard's life—there is nothing left untouched that may be salvaged. Similarly, when a person is filled with the Spirit, every aspect of his life is under the Spirit's influence; there are no areas that are untouched by Him. That does not mean the person filled with the Spirit is perfect, but it does mean that the Spirit is at work in the totality of his life. Preachers who preach to the heart are men who preach under the influence of the Spirit.

Preachers whose lives are filled with the Spirit are genuine; they are not hypocrites who lose preaching power because they harbor sin in certain areas of their lives. Because they, too, have been dealing with sin in all areas of their lives, they understand the problems of those to whom they preach. They preach with conviction because there is no area of life about which they fear to speak lest their preaching boomerang. They have already acknowledged their need for the Spirit to transform them totally and are asking Him to do so. Because they hold nothing back, they can preach with abandon. Moreover, having already experienced something of the Spirit's

---

2 According to Luke, a life under Satan's influence also can be said to be "filled": "Why has Satan filled your heart to lie to the Holy Spirit ...?" (Acts 5:3a).

pruning in every aspect of life, they are able to zero in on their listeners' problems in ways that could not be learned from textbooks alone. That too makes a difference in the way they preach.

If there is one emphasis found in the Book of Acts, it is the church's power in preaching, and that this power came from the filling of the Holy Spirit. There is no other way to explain the church's rapid growth. Times have changed, and so has preaching. But our God has not. Neither He nor the needs of men have been changed by the passing of time; sin and salvation, repentance and sanctification all remain the same. What has changed is that preachers today believe they do not need the filling of the Spirit, have a distorted view of what that filling is, or do not think it is possible. It is time we begin to reexamine the biblical teaching on the subject; then, perhaps, we would begin to experience power in our lives and in our preaching.

This filling of the Spirit is not some second work of grace. Rather, it is an ongoing work in which the Spirit more and more controls each area of our lives. It is the sanctification (the gradual process of putting off sin and replacing it with righteousness) of the whole man. It is a matter of asking the Spirit to work in every area of life and having a willingness to be changed by Him in anything, no matter what it may be. This is what Paul prayed for the Thessalonians: "May the God of peace Himself sanctify you completely; may your entire being—spirit and soul and body—be kept blameless for the coming of our Lord Jesus Christ" (1 Thess. 5:23).

The original worshipers on the day of Pentecost, together with those converted on that occasion, were genuinely Spirit-filled: "Every day they continued to meet in the temple in unity of spirit, and from house to house they broke bread together, sharing meals in gladness and *sincerity of heart*." They were *genuine*. It is not as though only the apostles and elders were filled with the Spirit; all who were present when the Spirit fell were filled (Acts 2:4). Yet, later on when the church wanted men fit to become deacons, it was necessary to "look for" men with "a good reputation, full of the Spirit and wisdom" (Acts 6:3). Presumably, by that time, not every believer was manifesting such a domination of the Spirit as all did at Pentecost (Acts 2:4), and so there was need to discriminate between those who were filled with the Spirit and those who were not.

It would seem that the original Pentecostal filling of the Spirit was an immediate, complete domination of the Spirit that caught up the 120 for that important occasion. But the Spirit's fullness was not to be automatically maintained. Pentecost was special; today, filling does not occur as an instant event in which we are passive. Rather, it is commanded (Eph. 5:18), indicating that we play a part in the process, and the verb in that verse makes it clear that filling is not a once-for-all event,[3] but must be nurtured by one's relationship to Christ. That is why, even by the time of Acts 6, it could be said that deacons must be selected only from among those who were filled with the Spirit (implying that not all were).

Tragically, today it cannot be said of every preacher in conservative churches (let alone deacons, elders, or members) that he is filled with the Spirit. This is the first problem. We must preach from the heart—a heart dominated by the Spirit—if we would preach to the hearts of others. But to preach from such a heart means that inwardly, day by day, we must experience the sanctifying work of the Spirit in every area of our lives. Preachers who do not preach with power to the hearts of men, therefore, should first examine their own hearts to be sure that the words of Peter and John addressed to Simon are not also appropriate to them: "You have no part or share in the proclamation of this message because your heart isn't right before God" (Acts 8:21). Clearly, all who wish to preach are not qualified to do so; the Word is to be proclaimed only by those whose hearts are right before God. Preaching is a heart-to-heart matter. When one's heart is right before God and he is a man after God's heart, he will be able to preach from heart to heart. Men like that will preach like the preachers in the Book of Acts.

---

[3] The tense of the verb in Ephesians 5:18, *plerousthe*, indicates a continual process, not a one-time or once-for-all event.

Chapter Four
Boldness of Heart

We are considering the question, "How does one preach to the heart?" and we have discovered thus far that the precondition for such preaching is a heart that is right with God. Power in preaching is an index of the fact that the preacher is filled with the Spirit. Only those whose hearts are right before God have any part in the proclamation of God's Word. Those who preach to the hearts of others, therefore, are those who have experienced the penetrating power of the sword of the Spirit thrust into their own hearts. They preach out of hearts that are dominated and influenced by the Spirit of God. They are preachers whose own hearts are aflame.

What does this do for a preacher? It gives him boldness in preaching.

If there is one characteristic that typifies modern preaching, it is its insipid, obsequious approach to speaking the truth. So unlike the early preachers, the Reformers, and the great preachers of all time, many modern Bible-believing preachers seem afraid to tell it like it is. And yet, that modern phrase, "tell it like it is," indicates that people generally appreciate hearing truth for what it is, even when what they hear isn't altogether pleasant. But it seems that in Christian circles, in particular, there is a pseudopious reserve or over-sophistication in which hypersensitive listeners are horrified by anything frank in preaching. There is, therefore, something wrong with modern preaching, and many of those who have been brought up on it, that must be corrected. It is basically a willingness to compromise—even God's truth—which stems from a lack of boldness.

I am not commending rudeness or crudeness. These unnecessary characteristics are often assumed to be synonymous with boldness. But there is nothing rude or crude about the preaching in the Book of Acts. The preaching found there is straightforward, clear, explicit, hard-hitting, and, in short, bold. In fact, the only feature of apostolic preaching described in Acts is its boldness.

Let's take a look at what Luke says about this matter and then at some of the preaching itself. The classic statement on the subject is found in the fourth chapter of Acts. There, the apostles and the people pray,

> "... So now, Lord, take note of their threats and give your slaves all the boldness needed to speak Your word" (Acts 4:29).

Verse 31 indicates that the prayer was answered and that they "spoke God's word boldly."

Even before this time, Luke notes that there was already a boldness about apostolic preaching that struck those who heard:

> Now when they saw the boldness of Peter and John and realized that they were uneducated laymen, they were surprised and recognized that they had been with Jesus (Acts 4:13).

Boldness, then, was considered a prerequisite for preaching and, when seen, was noted favorably. The same is true today, no less than it was in apostolic times: boldness is essential for preaching to the heart, and bold preaching makes an impact on those who hear.

It was said that when they saw the boldness of Peter and John, they recognized that "they had been with Jesus." The way some prissy Christians today look aghast at any boldness in preaching, you would think instead that a bold preacher had been with the Devil! Most people, however, recognize a truly bold preacher as an unusual man and are interested in him and often in what he has to say. One reason why much contemporary preaching not only fails to reach the heart, but is so uninteresting, is that it is timid and pale. Bold preaching is never dull.

What is boldness? The Greek word, *parresia*, means freedom in speaking, openness, willingness to be frank; it is plain speech that is unencumbered by fear. A bold preacher is one who has no fear of speaking the truth—even when it hurts. Many ministries are hampered today simply because of the fear of men. "Will Mrs. Jones take offense if I preach this?" "What will happen if I teach this to the congregation?" and similar thoughts go through the minds of far too many preachers when what they ought to be asking themselves is, "What will God think of me if I don't teach His truth?"

There is far too little teaching about judgment, hell, and the other doctrines on the dark side of the scriptural spectrum. There is too little reproving of sin. There is too little church discipline and confronting error, even when it is seriously affecting the membership of the church. There is a fear of controversy.

In some circles, the fear of controversy is so great that preachers, and congregations following after them, will settle for peace at any cost—even at the cost of truth, God's truth. The idea is that peace is all-important. Peace is a biblical ideal (Rom. 12:18 makes that clear: "If possible, so far as it depends on you, be at peace with everybody.")[1] , but so is purity. The peace of the church may never be bought at the cost of the purity of the church. That price is too dear. But why do we think that we can get along in this world, or for that matter, even in that church, without conflict and controversy? Jesus didn't. Paul didn't. None of the preachers of the apostolic age who faithfully served their Lord were spared controversy. Who are we to escape controversy when they did not? The story of the advance of the church across the Mediterranean world from Jerusalem to Rome is a story of controversy. When the gospel is preached boldly, there will be controversy. Most of the Epistles themselves were called forth to counter error of doctrine and sinfulness of life. In them there is controversy. Paul's life is a life of controversy. Tradition tells us that every apostle except John, who was exiled for his faith, died a violent death.

What is this hypersensitivity that is so often found among a particular brand of evangelicals today? Children around us grow up on TV and movies that feature not only conflict, but violence and crudity. Who in our age is so allergic to frankness that the open preaching of God's Word will cause him to break out in horror? Pale, insipid preaching is what drives people from Christ and the church, not bold preaching. It seems to me that the problem with hypersensitive evangelicals is not really the one stated up front—offending those to whom we preach—but, more often than not, simply a lack of boldness. And that lack of boldness boils down to a simple fear of men—fear of the consequences of telling it like it is.

Preachers are soldiers in a battle for Christ, Paul told Timothy. As faithful soldiers, fighting the good fight, they are to assault the walls of

---

1 The words, "if possible," show Paul's realism. Intransigent unbelief and disobedience on the part of others may make peace impossible when they hold out for what opposes God.

thought that men rear up against the gospel and take captives for Christ. They are also shepherds. As good shepherds, they are to drive wolves away from the flock and rescue those sheep that wander into dangerous places. A good shepherd carries not only a staff, but a rod (a mace used to drive off wild animals) and a sling (remember David's?). The images of the pastor/preacher are not images of men in soft clothing who never soil their hands; they are images of the hard-working farmer in his struggle against weeds, the soldier fighting the enemy, the shepherd protecting the sheep: they are images of conflict. If a minister of the gospel is afraid to "fight the good fight," he does not "keep the faith." So, in order to discharge his duties faithfully, he must be bold.

Boldness characterized the preaching of the apostles and other early preachers, Luke says. Let's take just a brief glimpse at a bit of their preaching. When the 3,000 were stung in their hearts, what sort of preaching was it that led to that? First of all, we see that it was preaching that did not hesitate to contradict the expressed ideas of men. Some said that the 120 who were speaking in foreign languages were drunk. But when Peter got up to preach, the very first words out of his mouth contradicted this foolish accusation: "Certainly these people aren't drunk, as you imagine; it's only nine o'clock in the morning!" (Acts 2:15). Well-meaning and fearful preachers will tell you that to openly contradict the audience is a poor preaching tactic—especially at the beginning of a sermon! But Peter had not read the experts; he simply relied on the Holy Spirit and went ahead speaking the truth. To win friends and influence people, you are supposed to begin by gaining agreement. However, Peter was more interested in the truth than in manipulating people through selling techniques.

Not only did Peter begin all wrong, according to the experts, but he was far too frank when he discussed his congregation's behavior. After all, Peter, it isn't polite to say such things as "this Man, delivered up by God's predetermined plan and foreknowledge, you killed by crucifixion!" (Acts 2:23). That sounds like a direct accusation, if not an attack on the audience. You'll never get anywhere that way, Peter. But Peter isn't finished. Listen to the conclusion: "So then, let the whole house of Israel know for certain that God has made this Jesus, Whom you crucified, both Lord and Christ." Now there you've done it, Peter! Just when it looked as if you might have pulled your sermon out of the fire after that opening blunder, you went ahead and spoiled everything by adding that last dig, "Whom you crucified." And, while I'm at it, let me tell you something else, Peter. You will never get anywhere using the second person in preaching; it's too personal. It is possible that you might have gotten away with saying everything you said—even those all-too-frank accusations—if you had only phrased them in the third person, in a more abstract way.

Now will Peter listen to reason? No, there he is in Acts 3, once again slinging around the second person and accosting his hearers with words like these: "Whom you delivered over and denied in front of Pilate …" (Acts 3:13[b]); "But you denied the Holy and Righteous One and asked for a murderer to be given to you …" (Acts 3:14); "So you killed the Author of life …" (Acts 3:15[a]). Peter, that sort of preaching certainly isn't calculated to win sermon prizes!

Well, when we listen to him in Acts 4, we see that Peter is never satisfied, never learns. There he is, at it again, as usual, using the second person and telling people in his typical, brassy manner how they have sinned: "Let all of you and all of the people of Israel know that it is by the name of Jesus Christ the Nazarene, Whom you crucified …" (Acts 4:10).

I guess it's hopeless trying to get anything across to Peter, and we won't even mention Stephen, with his aggressiveness: "You stiffnecked people, uncircumcised in hearts and ears! You always resist the Holy Spirit. As your fathers did, so do you!… they killed those who predicted the coming of the righteous One, of Whom you now have become the murderers and betrayers …" (Acts 7:51, 52). No, Stephen is also hopeless.

So, let's try Paul; he's a highly educated man. Can we expect a more refined approach from him? I'm not sure we are going to get very far there either. Look how he begins his preaching: "he preached boldly in Jesus' name … going in and out, preaching boldly in the Lord's name" (Acts 9:27-28). We've already seen what this boldness is like! Perhaps he will do better on his first missionary journey. Oh my, listen to him at Paphos, the very first place where we hear what he has to say: "You son of the devil, full of every kind of deceit and fraud, you enemy of every kind of righteousness; won't you ever stop making the Lord's straight roads crooked?" (Acts 13:10).[2] Paul,

---

2   Lest any hypersensitive brothers be offended by Paul's bold words, let me observe that these words are immediately preceded by this comment: "But Saul (who is called Paul), filled with the Holy Spirit, looked straight at him and said…"

that won't do. That sort of talk will get you in all sorts of trouble; why you might be thrown into prison, beaten, or even stoned!"

I won't go further. To do so would only multiply the obvious. Apostolic preachers were clear, personal, and direct; they were fearless. At times they were bold to the point of being blunt. Today, we need to be reminded of this. There is no denying the fact that, on the whole, today's mild preaching is very different; one might even call it antiseptic, by comparison. And so too are the results quite different. The reason for these differences is that today preachers lack boldness of heart.

As we have seen, the early church prayed for boldness, and the Spirit produced this boldness within them (Acts 4:29-31). That is the same way that preachers must acquire boldness today. When did you ask God to make you a bold preacher? When did you ask for "all the boldness needed to speak?" Are you afraid to ask? Do you fear the consequences of asking? After all, God might hear and answer your prayer! Then where would you be? Right, getting yourself into a lot of trouble, like Paul and Peter and Stephen! That would never do, would it? But, notice the interesting dilemma that I have just sketched: you are afraid to pray for boldness because you might get it, and you fear what would happen as a consequence. But don't you see the fallacy in that sort of reasoning? You would not fear any longer if you did become bold; as a matter of fact, you fear such consequences only because you *now* fear consequences. It will all change when the Lord answers your prayer.

Will God answer? Yes. As his record clearly shows, Peter was not always bold. Like a good father, God will not give you a snake or a scorpion if you ask for a fish or an egg. He even reasons with you about the matter: "So, then, if you who are evil know how to give good gifts to your children, how much more will the heavenly Father give the Holy Spirit to those who ask Him?" (Luke 11:11-13). The Spirit produces holy boldness; will you ask Him for it?

This boldness will not come in the form of a surge of feeling by which you will immediately recognize that it has been given to you. But, as you step forward in faith and obedience, again and again to speak with frankness and honesty, with directness and clarity, you will discover that the fear of man will have less and less influence on what you say. Pray, speak, and learn.

Chapter Five
Preaching from God's Heart

We have been thinking not only about what it means to preach to the heart, but also about how it is done. So far, we have discovered that the preacher himself must cultivate the right kind of heart so that he may preach in the power of the Holy Spirit with boldness. But what does he preach?

He preaches a message that comes from God's heart. This terminology, "God's heart," at first may trouble you as it did me. But then I discovered this year that in the Bible, God Himself does not hesitate to speak of His heart. For instance, He calls David, "a man after My own heart" (1 Sam. 13:14), meaning one who is in sympathy with His own thoughts and concerns. In Jeremiah, the notion of God's heart appears again and again: 3:15; 7:31; 19:5; 23:20; 30:24; 32:35, 41, often in speaking of some idea never having come into God's heart[1] (there, the meaning of heart as "thoughts" or "mind" is very clear). But, especially, Jeremiah speaks of the time when God says that He will provide "shepherds according to My heart, who will feed you knowledge and understanding" (Jer. 3:15). This passage is important to us.

The preachers God uses are men who are after (literally, "as") His heart. That is to say, they understand God's purposes and His ways, they are in harmony with them, and they are anxious to tell others about them. The concerns they have were first God's concerns. Such shepherds feed God's flock what He wants them to: "knowledge and understanding." Where do they get it? From His Word. Men who preach to the heart, then, are men who know God's Word, who personally accept and are molded by God's Word, and who, as a result, are capable of feeding others on that life-giving and nourishing Word. So, the preacher must be capable of understanding God's Word and feeding others on it.

A preacher who is filled with the Spirit is also filled with the Spirit's mes-

---

1 This, of course, is anthropomorphic language.

sage. He does not preach what he wants to preach; he preaches what the Spirit has caused to be written. In a peculiar sense, the Bible is the Spirit's Book. He carried its writers along, enabling them to write it error-free (2 Pet. 1:21); when Scripture is quoted, often we are told, as we are in Hebrews 3:7, "The Spirit says…"

Prophets sent from God frequently began their writings with words something like these: "The burden of the Word of the Lord to Israel by Malachi" (Mal. 1:1). What do those words mean? The Hebrew word translated "burden" means "something that is carried; a load." But because the Word of God was such a weighty thing for a man to carry to his fellow countrymen, this term was used of the prophetic message and, in time, came to mean "an oracle [especially a threatening one] from God."

The term never lost its idea of a burden or load to be borne. And it is exactly that fact that we must understand if we are to come to a full appreciation of what it means to preach to the heart. Sometimes we speak of "delivering" a message. That modern terminology fits quite well with the biblical notion of bearing a message. A preacher who thoroughly understands what he must say to his listeners, with all of its gravity and importance as the Word of God, goes into the pulpit weighed down with a burden. He has a burden on his heart. And it is not until he has accurately and faithfully conveyed that message to his listeners that he can truly be said to have "delivered" it. Because of the weight of responsibility involved in conveying God's Word to others, those who deliver it faithfully are also delivered of it. Only then is the weight of the responsibility lifted from their hearts. Men fail to preach to the heart when they do not feel that weight personally.

Paul experienced this weight. He tells us as much when he writes of himself as a "debtor" (Rom. 1:14) and when he cries out, "Woe to me if I don't announce the good news!" (1 Cor. 9:16^{b}). And something of that same necessity is discernible in the words of Peter and John: "We can't do anything but speak what we saw and heard" (Acts 4:20).

What is the message of the Lord that the preacher today must deliver? It consists of two elements: the gospel and the implications of the gospel in the lives of those who have believed it. The gospel is the news about the substitutionary, penal, sacrificial death of Christ for sinners and His bodily resurrection from the dead. The gospel's implications are all of those teachings Christ "commanded" His disciples to "observe" (Matt. 28:20). The preacher's twofold burden, therefore, is to proclaim a message of evangelism and sanctification.

The source of heart-reaching messages is the Bible. "Faith" comes from hearing the Word (Rom. 10:17). Prophets and apostles had direct revelation from God; today we have that same revelation in an inscripturated form. The idea of the written Word of God is not recent; it is biblical. The Bible calls itself God's Word (cf. esp. Ps. 119), despite what liberals confidently say to the contrary. So, if preachers wish not only to preach to the heart, but to preach in ways that are pleasing to God, they must preach "after [as] His heart." To do that, they must learn His thoughts and intents (heart) and become attuned to them in their own lives. They may learn from the Bible all that it is necessary to preach (cf. 2 Tim. 3:16-17). Indeed, there is only one way to preach to hearts: to preach from God's heart; but God has revealed His heart only in His written Word.

I shall not discuss how best to interpret the Bible; I have said much about that in *What to Do on Thursday, Preaching with Purpose*, and *Truth Apparent*, books in which I have stressed the need for *telic* preaching. The *telos* is the purpose of a preaching portion. Frequently, preachers use the Scriptures for their own purposes rather than for the purposes for which the Holy Spirit gave them, thereby losing the power to preach to hearts. *Telic* preachers concentrate on discovering the Holy Spirit's purpose in any given passage and make that purpose their own. They make sure they use the preaching portion for the same purpose or purposes for which it was given. They struggle with a passage until they know what the Holy Spirit intended to do to the reader by means of that passage, and they make that also the intention of their sermon. That is the way to discover and preach the heart of God. Only the one who knows His heart can become a shepherd who is after God's heart, feeding His flock on His knowledge and understanding. Precisely how one discovers the *telos* of a passage, what implications that *telos* has on other aspects of preaching, etc., is discussed in the books that I have mentioned at the beginning of this paragraph.

As important as illustrations and examples may be to make a biblical truth clear, memorable, and personal, they may never replace God's Word in preaching. Preachers who choose a theme and string illustrations along it like beads err greatly; they must learn, rather, to preach from the thoughts and mind of God. Paul asks, "Who knows the thoughts of a person except the spirit of the person in him?" Then, he points out, "So too no one knows God's thoughts except God's Spirit" (1 Cor. 2:11). And, in the Scriptures, he observes, "To us God revealed it by His Spirit. The Spirit searches into everything, even the deep thoughts of God" (v. 10). Because of the Spirit's revelation in the Scriptures, together with His illuminating power within the believer, Paul can declare, "… we have the mind of Christ" (v. 16).

How tragic, therefore, that men in the pulpit prattle on about the ideas of other men, share their own opinions, and feed God's sheep on diets of everything else. All the while, food provided by God—available, nourishing, life-giving—is almost totally neglected. Preacher, you will preach to the heart only when you preach from God's heart. You will preach from God's heart only when you know what is in His heart. And you will know what is in His heart only when you know His Word. You must dedicate yourself, therefore, to a thorough study of that Word so that you will truly become a workman in the Word who does not need to be ashamed, because you have accurately handled the Word of truth (2 Tim. 2:15) in your preaching.

Chapter Six
Heart-Convicting Preaching

Not all preaching involves conviction of sin. There is preaching that is primarily informative, preaching that brings encouragement and assistance to the listener, and preaching that lifts one's heart in doxology to God.[1] But, in this chapter, we are concerned with the sort of preaching that leads to conviction of sin.

We have seen that preaching to the heart is preaching in which the Holy Spirit is intimately involved. Because that is so, we must consider the matter of conviction. Jesus told us that "when He [the Spirit] comes, He will convict the world about sin, about righteousness and about judgment" (John 16:8). Since we must preach the gospel to the world, and it is the mission of the Holy Spirit to convict the world, the heart-piercing message that Peter preached is a message that convicts. But, as we have seen, the other aspect of the church's preaching is to the church itself; does it also include a message that convicts? Yes. There are any number of passages to which one might refer, but I would turn your attention only to the following: "All Scripture is breathed out by God and useful for teaching, for conviction, for correction and for disciplined training in righteousness" (2 Tim. 3:16). In preaching "the Word," Timothy is commanded, "Be at it in season and out of season. Convict, reprove, urge with complete patience and full teaching" (2 Tim. 4:2).

We must examine the term that is translated "convict" and then look in some detail at the verses that have just been mentioned. But, before we do, let me point out once more, as Paul does in writing to Timothy, that listeners will

---
1 But even in this sort of preaching, where the emphasis is on something else, the need for conviction is frequently present. How can one praise God, and at the same time not be reminded of his own unworthiness? The need for encouragement and assistance often points to one's failure to seek out the same sooner, or to his lack of diligence in doing so. New information leads to new responsibilities and the recognition of sin previously unknown.

be "convicted" when the Scriptures are preached. The God-breathed Scriptures are the means that the Spirit uses to convict the listener because they are the source of His message. Preachers should not depend on haranguing, the use of sob stories, and the like to bring about conviction; rather, they must depend upon a faithful proclamation of biblical truth to do the job. The Spirit uses His Word, as it is faithfully preached, to convict of sin.

Let us consider, then, the term that is translated "convict." Some versions read "rebuke" or "reprove" instead of "convict." These translations are too weak. The Holy Spirit does not merely make charges; He fully substantiates them. The term *elengcho* comes from the law courts. It means not only to prefer charges, but also to so pursue the case against the one who is charged that he is *convicted* of the crime of which he is accused. The one who convicts *proves another guilty*. The Holy Spirit is our lawyer (*parakletos* = lawyer). He defends us from Satan, the accuser of the brethren. He pleads the blood of Christ before the judgment throne of God. But He is not only our defense attorney, our counselor-at-law; He is also the prosecuting attorney, bringing the case against those who must be convicted. So, the term means, then, to prove a charge.

That is what Jesus had in mind when He said that the Holy Spirit would "convict the world about sin, about righteousness and about judgment" (John 16:8). The Holy Spirit has come to make His case, and when He finishes doing so, men stand exposed for what they are. He cuts through all of the fog and confusion and brings conviction by His Word that what He has charged is correct.

Now, Jesus explains the Spirit's case against the world. He takes each of the three elements in the case and extrapolates on it. He says:

> ... about sin—because they don't believe in Me, about righteousness—because I am going to My Father and you won't see Me any more, and about judgment—because this world's ruler has been judged (John 16:9-11).

Just what does He mean by these explanations?

The Spirit will convict the world (in John's writings, *world* frequently is used to refer to Gentiles as well as Jews, in contrast to Jews only). His activities will be worldwide in scope. Commenting on this passage, Calvin asks, "For how comes it that the voice proceeding from the mouth of a man [in preaching] penetrates into hearts, takes root there, and at length yields fruit, changing hearts of stone into hearts of flesh, and renewing men, but because the Spirit of Christ quickens it?" As Hendriksen puts it, He came to "publicly *expose its guilt and call it to repentance.*"

His case against the world involves three things: sin, righteousness, and judgment. He proves His case by affirming the sin of the world, which is clearly evidenced in its unbelief, by demonstrating the righteousness of Christ, which is plainly proved in His resurrection and ascension, and by declaring the dethronement of the Devil, which is unmistakably implied in his judgment on the cross. This case is foolproof; the world has no answer to it. It constitutes the biblical message of the gospel: Christ came to die for sinners, rose from the dead, and defeated the evil one.

But the Spirit also convicts the church of sin. Sanctification is a process that often involves such conviction. That process is set forth in 2 Timothy 3:16. There, four elements stand out: the Scriptures are useful for (1) teaching, (2) *conviction*, (3) correction, and (4) disciplined training in righteousness. That is to say, the preacher uses the Bible (v. 17) to teach God's standards, to show us how we have failed to measure up to them, to tell us how to get ourselves out of the messes we get ourselves into because of our sins, and to help us avoid falling into the same sins again in the future. Conviction comes from teaching God's truth about His requirements for believers and about how our failure to live according to them displeases the Savior who died for them.

When Paul wrote, "Preach the Word… Convict, reprove, urge with complete patience and full teaching," he was saying practically the same thing. Surely, in some pulpits today, there is far too little preaching that convicts and rebukes. In others, there is rebuking enough, but there is little or no patience with people, and often very little teaching about precisely what changes God requires and how to make them. It is very likely that the verb translated "urge" might better be translated "assist" (*parakaleo* has that more general meaning in most passages and refers to doing or saying whatever is necessary to help another accomplish something). Certainly, if it is a fault of some preachers not to rebuke, it is a fault of many others who, having rebuked, fail to help their listeners make the necessary changes. (For more on implementation of one's teaching, see *What to Do on Thursday* and *Preaching with Purpose.*)

So, both unbelievers and believers need to experience the penetrating power of the Word as it cuts through to the heart. The writer of Hebrews spoke of this power of the Word. Here is what he said:

> *God's Word is alive and active, sharper than any two-edged sword, penetrating deeply enough to cut open soul and spirit and joints and marrow; it can judge the desires and thoughts of the heart. And before Him no creature can hide, but all are naked and vulnerable to the eyes of Him to Whom we must give an account (Heb. 4:12-13).*

There is a description, under the figure of a sword, of the Bible's power to penetrate to the deepest recesses of the heart. There is nothing in a man's life that the Scriptures cannot touch, no area that can escape their probing thrust. The Scriptures are entirely adequate to convict of any and every sin. The Bible strips us of all our defenses and cuts us open before God's eyes like fallen warriors, totally vulnerable. It lays open the soul and the spirit (not divides between them, as some wrongly interpret); it discloses both the thoughts and the desires of the heart. No man can stand before it, claiming his innocence. It convicts; the Spirit uses His written Word as it is preached to pierce through to men's hearts.

But there will be no conviction of sin unless the Word is used, and used properly. That means that it will be used boldly, appropriately, and fully as Paul used it when he reminded the Ephesian elders,

> *I didn't hold back in declaring anything that was beneficial to you....; I haven't held back in declaring God's whole counsel to you"* (Acts 20:20, 27).

There is often a tendency for a preacher to "hold back" precisely what may benefit the congregation, for fear that he may get himself in trouble. The result is that the whole counsel of God is not proclaimed. Hard truths are either bypassed or soft-pedaled. Unpopular doctrines, if preached at all, are served in such small quantities or in such a diluted form that they could hardly be described as that sort of "healthy [i.e., health-promoting] teaching" that Paul required of preachers when writing to Timothy. But the tendency of preachers to hold back is dangerous. Paul said, "So then, I testify to you this day that I am clean from everybody's blood because I haven't held back

...." (Acts 20:26-27). Clearly, those who hold back are not. No wonder James warned, "My brothers, not many of you should be teachers, because you know that we teachers will receive stricter judgment" (James 3:1).

Preacher, do you preach the Word in order to gain conviction? Do you preach the Word with all of its inherent force and power? Do you preach all of the Word, or only those portions that you think will be readily acceptable to your hearers? Is anyone's blood on your head?

Chapter Seven
A Heart-Adapted Form

We have seen how necessary it is to preach boldly the whole counsel of God in the power of the Spirit in order to bring conviction. But, at the close of the last chapter, I began to mention another matter—form. There are a number of ways in which those who do care to proclaim God's truth boldly nevertheless do fail—largely because of poor form. In this chapter, we shall discuss this matter in depth.

In Colossians 4:3-4, Paul wrote:

> *... praying at the same time also about us, that God may open for us a door for the Word, to speak about the secret of Christ, because of which I am in bonds, so that I may proclaim it clearly, as I ought to.*

To "proclaim it clearly, as I ought to"—those words have to do with form.

Sometimes, those who would be "more pious than Paul" try to tell us that form is unimportant. So long as the truth is proclaimed, what more is there to do? It is God's Word, they say, not our eloquence, that gets the job done. There are both truth and error in those statements.

Of course it is not our eloquence that changes people. Paul made that point in 1 Corinthians 2:1-5. But here, in Colossians, Paul is so deeply concerned about clarity (a matter of form) that he urges the Colossian church to pray about the matter. Does Paul contradict himself—in one place denouncing those who focus on form and, in another, stressing its importance? No, there is no contradiction. Eloquence was not Paul's concern. He told the Corinthians that he wanted their faith to rest only on the power of the Spirit; he did not want them drawn into some false profession of faith based on the clever rhetoric of men. Studied eloquence, rhetorical gimmicks, and the like are to be scrapped. But that does not mean all concern about form must be avoided. Paul was not interested in becoming a Demosthenes, but his aim was to preach in a *form that is appropriate to the message*. Notice, his concern is for clarity. That, as I said, is a matter of form. And his comment is that the preacher is obligated to be clear ("as I *ought* to" speak). The desire to be clear and the desire to be eloquent are two entirely different things.

Paul's one goal was to avoid anything that might obscure God's truth and to do everything that he could to present it as clearly as possible. There is no contradiction between that desire and an unwillingness to have his listeners' faith depend upon something other than the gospel of Christ. In fact, the two concerns dovetail: if anything obscures the gospel, it isn't possible for people to understand and believe it. Preacher, that means that you must not seek to become a Demosthenes, calling attention to your rhetorical powers, but you must do whatever is necessary to be sure that your proclamation of the convicting, nourishing Word is clear. You must aim not at the applause of men, but at reaching their hearts.

Clarity is the one prerequisite pertaining to form that is essential to preaching to the heart. How sad it is that preachers do not work more on this matter of clarity. How important it must be if the apostle Paul himself was concerned enough about it to ask for prayer. Have you ever asked your congregation to pray for clarity in your preaching? Have you ever asked them to pray about your preaching at all?

Terminology can obscure. The great theological words of the Bible cannot be abandoned, but neither should they be preached without clear definition. I do not mean that you must always say, in so many words, "Justification is...." No, often, having used the word, you may include a definition in the same sentence: "If you believe, God will justify you, declaring you righteous and counting you perfect in His sight."

There are, however, many terms that might be reserved for teaching in more explicitly doctrinal settings. Words like eschatology and soteriology do not need to be used in the pulpit. Yet, some men, perhaps thinking that they will be viewed as erudite, constantly use language that hinders rather than facilitates the presentation of the message. Others, whose hearts may be right, simply carry the language of the seminaries and the commentaries over into the pulpit. This too is a mistake.

Sometimes the cultivation of a "preaching style" with its quasi-Elizabethan language obscures. A wall plaque reads, "ESCHEW OBFUSCATION." It might be good to print your own copy and keep it under the glass on the desk in the study. Obviously, the word "obfuscation" raises a flag against all stilted, technical, or otherwise unclear modern terminology, while the word "eschew" pokes fun at outdated and archaic terms. This "preaching style" seems to relish such vocabulary. You may find that you will have to spend time studying your own usage in order to discover whether you are guilty of obscuring the truth when you preach. The New Testament was largely written by simple men using the street language of the day. Paul, a highly educated man, found it necessary to work at not allowing his educational habits to get in the way of clarity in preaching. You will have to do the same.

Of course, there are many preachers whose grammar is incorrect and whose syntax is sloppy. They have never learned how to speak plainly and accurately. While stressing clarity, the Bible puts no premium on sloppiness. Indeed, sloppy grammar and syntax tend to obscure. People find themselves saying, "Did he mean this ... or that?" Clarity is a matter of simplicity rather than ornateness; it consists of plainness of speech rather than eloquence or eruditeness, and it focuses on accuracy of grammar and syntax rather than sloppiness.

How effective is your preaching style? If it is defective in one or more of these ways, your style may get in the way of the message and keep it from penetrating your listener's heart. It will matter little how much preparation you may have done to obtain the finest food to feed the flock; it will not make much difference whether you present your message boldly or not; if what you have to say is unclear, everything you do may be in vain. Clarity is the thing. Paul was right—that is how he was to speak; preacher, it is also how you ought to speak.

Conclusion

You have been faced with a challenge. In this short book I have not attempted to treat every aspect of the subject, but only those which might, in a practical way, challenge you to thought and deeper commitment. You know better than anyone else what deficiencies there are in your preaching. It is my prayer that this book will not only stir you again to the hope of preaching to hearts with power, but also to act on that hope.

Now that you know what is required, what will you do about it? Filled with good intentions, will you put down the book and allow yourself to be caught up in the many other affairs that make demands on you, never to go beyond hopes and good resolutions? That is what your congregation so often does after you have preached effectively and reached their hearts. Will you follow their lead, or will you be a leader who, himself, is able to demonstrate that he is capable of doing differently?

If the words of this book have reached your heart, admit it to yourself. Tell God about it, and then lay out a plan for doing what must be done to effect the needed changes. It is my observation that unless busy people determine exactly what must be done and then set out a schedule for doing it, little will be accomplished. Making the changes that are necessary for preaching to the heart will take some time and effort—especially regular, disciplined effort. Changes will not be made, therefore, unless there is a commitment to make them, coupled with a plan for bringing them about. Are you willing to listen to the conviction of your heart?

If so, let me suggest that you get a notebook and lay out that plan. You will want more specific help, such as that which is found in *Preaching with Purpose*, an earlier textbook on preaching, written with the intention of giving just such help to those who need it. Put down all that you need to do, and *date each element in your plan*. May the God of all grace give you great grace as He enables you to work at becoming a preacher of the Word to the hearts of men!

Communicating With 20th Century Man

Preface

There has been too little good communication by the church with the world around us. It is time we became concerned about this matter and did something about it.

This short monograph was designed to challenge leaders (and leaders to be) in the contemporary church to become aware of the problem and to seek out personal and corporate solutions to it.

I hope the book will be widely read by pastors, seminary and Bible college students, as well as concerned church leaders everywhere.

There are few concrete solutions here. This book is more of an analysis of the present situation and its many problems, along with pointers to the way out of them. More concrete suggestions may be found in my series of articles on communication in The Journal of Pastoral Practice.

Here I am making a plea—one that I pray will be heard and heeded. I make it because so little has been (and is being) said of value on this topic.

In a day in which the world has learned so much about good communication (though what it communicates isn't so good), the church dare not lag behind. Inasmuch as we do lag behind in poor communication, the blame does not rest on our message, but on how we express it. It is time we do something about that problem.

Chapter One
The Signs of the Times

I hope that you will find the topic of this book both interesting and timely. It is "Communicating with 20th Century Man."

At the start, there are at least two things I am sure you will want to hear something about before we can go further:

1. What is meant by "20th Century Man"?
2. To what does the word "communication" refer?

Definition and *delimitation* of these two subjects will lead directly to the main theme, which itself may be stated in the form of a third question:

3. What principles may be accepted and what *techniques* may be employed in communicating with 20th Century Man?

Obviously, no such creature as "20th Century Man" exists in pure form. People are individuals. Like snowflakes, no two are exactly alike. Strictly speaking, there is no such thing as "man." There are only men, so there is no 20th Century Man. Hereditary, environmental, cultural, geographical, political, and above all, theological differences in an almost infinite variety of combinations assure pluriformity. The old quip is that "every generalization is inaccurate—including this one." Few statements could more aptly describe the problem of generalizing about the most complex and diversified creature of God-man.

However, so long as one recognizes what it is, one may sketch a general, composite image of humanity from the current drift of human thought. The modern preacher who wishes to communicate the gospel more effectively may find such a sketch helpful. Man reveals his thoughts in social, economic, political, philosophical, scientific, and ecclesiastical writings and actions. As these change from era to era, man's image changes too. If you recognize that there are many notable exceptions, and that this composite image is somewhat artificial, it will be safe to proceed to a consideration of "20th Century Man" after we have made another delimitation.

Diversity is not the only difficulty. The topic itself—"20th Century Man"—is, in one sense, too broad. Thus far there have been two distinct images of man in this 20th century. Who knows how many more may appear before it's close. Already 20th Century Man has radically changed his viewpoint, goals, and attitudes. This change, in fact, amounts almost to a complete reversal. In 1960, William C. DeVane, dean of Yale College, himself a member of the graduating class of 1920, sketched a contrasting portrait of the graduate of his era and today's graduates. In 1920, he says, the Yale undergraduate

> was far more assured than his present counterpart … He was a tough-minded, self-contained, unconscious young snob [who] still had faith in his world … It was bliss in that dawn to be alive, but it was the bliss that one sometimes feels between sleep and waking.

Of the present-day graduate he says,

> He has a deep well of skepticism in him—the advertisers, psychologists, television quiz champions, and politicians have seen to that.[1]

People in the initial years of the 20th century placed great faith in man. They were idealistic and optimistic about his future. In the middle years, they have shared quite the opposite opinion of him. Distrust and fear of man prevailed. Writers became disillusioned and pessimistic about man. Now, although it is too early to say, there may be a further turning on the part of some to a new optimism. The image of "20th Century Man" is, therefore, already twofold depending upon which of these periods one is discussing.

The first few years of this century saw a continuation of the spirit that characterized human thinking during the latter half of the 19th century. Thus historians might say contemporary man was merely in the making during the beginning of the 20th century. At any rate, for my purpose (which is practical), it is more important to understand contemporary (period two) man since we are interested in improving communication with him. Thus, throughout this discussion, the phrase "20th Century Man" means man in his contemporary image. This designation, then, refers not to *idealistic* man, but to *disillusioned* man. Interest in man in the earlier state concerns how that state throws light upon his present condition (by reaction, overaction, etc.). We cannot avoid discussing why contemporary man is what he is.

---

1 *Newsweek*, May 9, 1960.

That 20th Century Man may be characterized most aptly as disillusioned, in itself is significant. In order to communicate successfully with him, the Christian must take this fully into account. There is a good reason to ask how man got into his present condition because his disillusionment is disillusionment over earlier expectations that failed. Answering that question is the first step toward discovering the means by which he may be reached with the message of hope. Knowing the cause of an illness is one pathway to its cure.

To begin with, the old optimistic era had its roots in rationalistic philosophy and evolutionary thought. The tenets of these movements were applied by scientists, philosophers, politicians, and theologians to their respective fields; they permeated all of life. Evolution anticipated a gradual improvement leading to a golden future for man. Rationalism enthroned man's reason and declared that as the result of human effort alone this glorious day would dawn. One understands why yesterday's Yale graduate was a cocky, self-confident young snob. Secure, with his faith anchored firmly to man, he went out to subdue the world through science, education, and social betterment. Casting off all authorities and standards, he consciously made man the measure of all things. His deification of man was naive. He honestly believed in the innate goodness of man. He believed that if man could be educated, encouraged, and employed, his own potential would be sufficient to place him on the throne.

In theology, evolutionists challenged traditional concepts. By and large, the church responded by extremes. Some capitulated altogether; others went the way of irresponsible obscurantism. Liberals applied rationalistic and naturalistic principles to Christian teaching, loosening it from its supernaturalistic moorings. They "explained away" all that opposed the current of the times. As a consequence, they left man with little more than an empty shell from which the kernel had been extracted. In the *name* of Christianity the theme was anything goes, so long as it sails under the flag of progressive, modern thought. Idealism in that age reigned supreme.

Then came the shock. Suddenly, the huge, monolithic structure fell apart! All its internal hollowness was finally exposed. Like giant hammer blows, first one, then a second, then a third and fourth horrible war, pounded the idealistic vision to smithereens. The basic brutality and inhumanity of man that these wars so clearly revealed, no longer could be denied, ignored, or sugar-coated. Down the drain went shattered hopes and dreams. A generation of disillusioned youth protested, many refusing to serve in Vietnam. A blighting depression in the 30's followed more recently by a runaway inflation plus devaluation served to reemphasize human tragedy. Faith in man's intellect and intrinsic goodness vanished like smoke. The nuclear threat hovering over all provides the assurance that disillusionment will hold a permanent place for some time to come.

Human destiny now *seems* to hang upon the future actions of irresponsible, discredited, and untrustworthy politicians. This fact has generated a prevailing worldwide atmosphere of gloom and despair. On top of it all came Watergate! Yes, two eras could hardly be more opposite!

And yet, while sensible people might conclude that all this at last would bring man to his knees before God, this has hardly been the result. While man is on his knees, once more he has enshrined new gods to whom he now vainly prays. But the very nature of these gods shows that even his prayers are but whistling in the dark. He does not really believe in these gods—certainly not as his fathers passionately believed in the gods of humanism and materialism.

The vanity of our new gods has been manifested in existential philosophy. Existentialists want to understand man in the midst of his tragedy. The sum of their thinking seems to amount to a sort of stoical determination to accept life honestly for what it is, even if nothing can be done to solve its terrible problems. Thus purpose (if the goal of existentialism can be expressed by so elevated a term) is best realized by living authentically. This means recognizing that all of life's despair hopelessly culminates in death. Stoic honesty, then, is the god of philosophic existentialism. But he is not a god of hope.

World statesmen have nothing better to offer. With less than hope against hope they confer and disagree. They once expressed dim hopes that the United Nations, or some plan for world government might succeed in bringing peace. But they do not really believe it will come. Now one hardly even hears of the United Nations.

"Scientism," once self-assured, also has been thrust from its lofty perch. Even its most staunch devotees now hiss and wag the head at it for the creation of a nuclear Frankenstein over which it has no control. People are afraid of science with its brainwashing and cloning capabilities. On the other hand, with a new sort of humility, some of its leaders admit the dilemma. They know man's present capabilities for mass destruction and control of human life better than the rest of us, and tremble. They also know they will bequeath to their children even more ghastly possibilities for destruction. But, in spite of all, so few embrace the gospel of Christ.

Worst of all, popular theologians today, instead of turning back to the one standard of hope and certainty, have spun tales of new gods about whom we can really know nothing except what we may discover in existential encounters or transcendental meditation. Irrationalism now prevails; feeling and experience orientations are dominant. Eastern religions get a hearing.

There is, to be sure, among some a new acknowledgment of sin and tension which the old (period-one) liberalism disavowed. But it is significant that in the voluminous amount of contemporary theological writing (vividly describing man's predicament), no one comes even near to offering a way out of that predicament. Even the most famous turn-of-the-era theologian admitted his own hopelessness. Karl Barth wrote:

> They have no answer to this question of questions, but are naive enough to assume others may have. So they thrust us into our anomalous profession and put us into their pulpits and professorial chairs, that we may tell them about God and give them the answer to their question no better than they themselves (The Word of God and the Word of Man, p. 187).

Neo-orthodox theologians (where they still exist) view the existential encounter as the medium of divine revelation. For them, revelation is not a deposit of factual data, but rather an event. But it is an experience that offers little tangible hope. In the final analysis, after all the learned theological and philosophical jargon has been stripped away, neo-orthodoxy leaves man in the same old morass of subjectivism that rationalism did. With no other final norm than himself (in a day in which he no longer has *confidence* in himself), neo-orthodoxy calls man to exercise blind faith in a subjective experience. Even this is unsure; there are no standard rituals whereby the existential moment may be induced. One must wait for it to "find" him. Having no other hope, modern religious man stands waiting, hoping against hope—knowingly on the brink of destruction—but helpless to do anything about it. In another day, a day of faith in man, Schleiermacher's subjectivism appealed. It took years for men to discover its basic unsoundness. But today, man is not going to fall into the same abyss. It has not taken him long to recognize the fact that this is nothing more than the same vapid subjectivism under a thin new veil. That is one reason that by now, existential neo-orthodoxy has all but dried up on the vine.

And so, in all areas of life the same spirit of helplessness prevails. Why is it that society has sunk so deeply into despair? Is it simply a result of historical circumstances? Not altogether. Undoubtedly, there has been the inevitable pendulum reaction. The pricked bubble of anticipated human achievement that the past generation so glibly fed its children, hardly could be the diet now fed to the next. There has been too much bitterness and disappointment for that. But there is more to be said. A large share of blame for the present world predicament must be laid at the doorstep of conservative Christianity. And the very point at which conservatives have failed most seriously is in the realm of communication.

It is not so much that they have been unaware of world developments, or have lacked the desire or zeal to spread the gospel. Nor is there any deficiency in the message that they have to communicate. The failure lies partly in the direction of outmoded methods of communication. Unbelievable as it may seem, King James English with its "brethren" (instead of "brothers") and "beloved" (instead of "dear friends"), still pervades the pulpit. Serious efforts to study and attempt new forms of preaching, even in some minor issues as word usage and vocabulary, have been meager. But beyond this, failure lies in the basic attitude of Christians toward contemporary times. We have become infected with the disease of contemporary man rather than his healers. We have *been influenced* more than we have *influenced*. We have been eclectic recipients rather than communicators. In short, conservative Christians have become worldly. Worldliness is epitomized by allowing the world's attitudes, opinions, and goals to influence the Christian's thinking. When the world makes more of an impact upon the church than the church upon the world, she is always at fault. And she may at once begin to ask herself (among other things), Why has the world's communication to me been so effective and mine to it so ineffective?

The answer to the problem is, of course, manifold. Spiritual lacks and weaknesses are undoubtedly at the core. Methodological ineptness is but a symptom of the sickness. The disease cannot be cured by treating its symptoms. Bad practice, Christians know, ultimately can be traced to poor doctrine.

What doctrinal error, then, is at the heart of the church's problems of communication? To a great extent it may be traced to an attitude created by a deemphasis upon the sovereignty of God. That full-orbed teaching of the Reformation leads inevitably to a strong, virile, aggressive church militant. But such a spirit today is almost nonexistent among conservative Christians. They have gone on the defensive, rather than assuming the offensive. Weak, watered-down theology of the type which overemphasizes anthropology—in a day in which man's capabilities are seriously questioned--has very little to offer a world *sick* of man. It does (of course) just as little for the church.

From this has grown a pessimistic eschatological attitude in which conservative prophets of doom chime in with the dying gasps of the neo-orthodox and with the howls of the skeptical chorus chanting humanity's funeral song. Such an attitude of hopeless futility has all but dissipated the aggressive outlook and outreach of conservativism. No wonder communication has broken down.

Away with this irresponsible talk of the proximate end of all things! Away with the gloomy spirit of hopelessness and despair among true believers! We can well leave that to the world with its subjective philosophies and theologies! It should not be named among the elect. All such despair is *totally without foundation*. God is sovereign; all is well.

Moreover, the emphasis of the Scriptures is upon the fact that before the coming of Christ and the end of the world, human society will be secure. A period such as the one which has just passed—not one like the present—again must emerge. It is when the world thinks it has it made and says "peace and safety" that "sudden destruction will come" (1 Thess. 5). The return of Christ will not take place in a time of worldwide fear and despair. It will occur in days like those of Lot and Noah, when people securely go about their own business blissfully oblivious of the tragedies and realities of life and death.

Christians have been blindfolded to the biblical facts, hoodwinked by the devil into a state of spiritual despair. Conservative prophets have erroneously characterized our times as a period of hopeless apostasy. They have pictured the church with its hands tied and almost all of her efforts doomed to certain failure. Nothing could be further from the truth. This is not a period of impossible apostasy. Everywhere men are more sympathetic toward the truth than they have been for generations. The awful final rebellion will come during a time of false safety and security, not when the world is shaking with anxiety and dread.

New Testament days in some ways were much like our own. That too was a time of breakdown of the old institutions. Faith in the man-made religions of Hellenistic society had long since been destroyed. Poets openly jeered at the gods of the pantheon. "Eternal Rome" had already begun to quake as the *Pax Romana* was disturbed by internal strife and external "wars and rumors of wars." It was a period of almost unparalleled moral degradation and all the *oikumene* was apprehensive in its unrest. People feared and wondered and longed with a soul hunger nothing human could satisfy. To such a society—one destitute of all that really mattered—the gospel went forth. And upon the wreckage of the past, it spread like a warm, wonderful blanket, bringing a hope and purpose to life that many doubted could ever be found. The unequaled response of that generation of yearning souls is now an indelible page in history. Why have today's children of Paul, Peter, and John failed to learn their great lesson? Are not the times ripe for history to repeat itself?

Granted, this is an age of darkness, but has true Christianity ever been afraid of the dark? Like a lamp, designed for that very purpose, she has always shone, most brilliantly in the dark. That is her task—to become the light of the world. Her light must glow brightly today, pointing lost wayfarers to the path of life. Founded upon the Rock, she is to stand a secure refuge in the storm, when all else is being swept away. Is this a time of despair, angst, dread, and helplessness for the church of Jesus Christ? No. Never. This is her hour. This is the day of opportunity for which she exists. This is the time for her to rise up in strength and demonstrate to all the world what Jesus Christ can do for a human life, for a nation, for a world!

The times cry loudly for a strong crystal note of authority. Confused and muddled, 20th Century Man is looking—longing—for answers and guidance. He is yearning for a sovereign God. He wants to know that there is purpose and control (beyond *human* purpose and control) in the universe. In the midst of human chaos, the church dare not represent God, too, as being confused and powerless. Yet as the world looks on today what does it so often see? A church floundering, just like the rest of society—defeated and defensive, satisfied to barely hold her own.

Communication with 20th Century Man, therefore, must begin with Christian convictions and attitudes. Therefore, the first and perhaps most important exhortation concerns the Christian's attitude toward the plight of 20th Century Man and the power of a sovereign God to do something about it. You will never succeed in communicating the gospel unless first you are confident that there can be success in doing so. Whether it be in Korea, Germany, Guatemala, or America, this fundamental principle holds true. For the glory of God, for the sake of the church, for the hope of 20th Century Man, help bring a halt to this eclectic worldliness. Determine that as one member of the church of Christ, you will not succumb to the spirit of the age. Instead, make it your purpose to go forth aggressively in this day of unparalleled opportunity. Make good use of every moment so long as that opportunity remains.

That ours truly is a time of unparalleled opportunity by now should be evident. This is not only demonstrated by the principle that Christianity shines brightest on the darkest nights. Mounting contemporary evidence likewise illustrates the truth of the assertion. Wherever pessimism has been replaced by an aggressive propagation of the gospel, it has found fertile soil. Take one example. Whatever one thinks of Billy Graham's theology or methods, one thing should be patent. He has demonstrated beyond question that conservative Christianity is well received in every part of the world today. Billy Graham has been successful—in spite of all his deficiencies—because, unlike so many of his critics, he believes in the possibility (as he puts it) of "revival in our time." His whole personality is permeated by this conviction. As people have listened to him proclaim the gospel in England, in America, in Africa, or in Australia, out of the midst of their own tragic existence, hope emerges—hope not only for eternity, but hope for the present. The tragedy is that while Graham, as an independent, has taken this stance, the church as a whole has not. Such aggressive, militant Christianity by the church alone can successfully communicate with the world that will accept nothing less than a sure hope by which contemporary despair can be superseded.

Ah no, this is not a new idealism. This is Christianity undefeated. This is the realistic Christian worldview for our time. It is not an idealism naively ignorant of the stark tragedies of 20th-century civilization. It is not a self-deceiving pair of rose-colored spectacles by which one attempts to transform ugliness into beauty. No, the Christian is a realist who clearly sees 20th Century Man in his sinful dilemma, recognizes the tragedy and peril, and knows that his own task is not easy. But, more fundamentally, he also believes that God is sovereign, and he recognizes what God has said about the possibilities of such an age. He knows that, with the God of Elijah, revival is not impossible even in *these* times. As a result, with prayerful hope and zeal, he sets out to build anew the altar of the Lord which has been broken down. He believes the fire of the Lord can fall again today! Perhaps the distinguishing feature among contemporary Christians and churches is the presence or lack of this Elijah spirit. It is impossible to speak of communication at all until this problem is faced; the conviction that communication is *worthwhile* and *possible* is basic to all else.

Yes, the world is ready for aggressive conservative Christianity. It might almost be said that 20th Century Man has newly acquired a fundamentalist attitude. He is interested in the basic or fundamental issues of being, life, death, and existence. Intellectually expressed, this attitude as first seen in modern existentialist philosophy's preoccupation with these very themes. Betrayed by man, man is now searching among the ruins for some other god in which to place his trust. Philosophy, neo-orthodoxy, science, and international politics have all been shown to be bereft of trustworthiness. Each, in its own area, can do little more than describe the world predicament. No really serious solutions are offered. The few who honestly believe that this mere analysis is itself a solution are only kidding themselves. Few there are who actually entertain such hope.

An additional indication of the spirit of the times, and the resultant opportunity which this affords true Christians, is the phenomenal rise of cults and the widespread advance of occultism. If there is one thing true of these movements, it is the fact that both offer concrete answers to life's deepest problems. There is nothing vague or subjective about the Jehovah's Witness, the "Moony," and the 7th Day Adventist. Each comes with all of the answers—and all the answers to the answers.

While true Christians do not gullibly swallow a party line as the cults do, they too have answers: biblical answers, God's answers. There is abundant evidence today that the groups with specific information to offer concerning life's great issues are the ones that receive a welcome response. True Christianity alone *has* these answers; why does she sit in despair, convinced that it is hardly worthwhile to try to communicate them?

Obviously, there is at least one other variation within the image of 20th Century Man that should be mentioned. In any era, the image varies to some extent, depending on whether one is discussing the attitudes and ideas of the intelligentsia or the masses. Traditionally, the former have been quicker to sense trends and therefore set the mood for the latter. It usually takes the masses a while to "catch up." Then, they ordinarily retain it a bit longer.

The advent of modern media of communication, such as television and radio, however, has had a great leveling effect so that the time lapse between when the eggheads get hold of an idea and when it is communicated to the masses in popular forms has become minimal and therefore of little consequence. But for what it is worth, it should be mentioned, and this interesting fact should be noted: The in-college student is probably the best standard, since he is still in touch with each sector of society and is strongly influenced by both. He is always in transition from the mass image to the intellectual image of the day. That is why I would like to tell you about a personal experience I had not too long ago.

I had the opportunity to speak during a Religious Emphasis Week at a large state university. The theme of the conference was "Religion for the Tough-Minded." It didn't take long to discover that whoever thought up that topic had entirely misjudged the spirit of the university student. Tough-minded students were at a premium. In fact, they were as tender-minded a bunch as I have ever met. That week, I spoke to nearly 1000 students during two-and-one-half-hour dorm discussions, personal interviews, and dinner engagements, but in all that time, among all of those young people, I received not one jeering question, and I didn't encounter a single heckler. Instead, I found students without a worldview—and who *knew* it! They complained of studying subjects in isolation and to no purpose. They sensed the lack of an underlying cohesion. They were anxious to discuss the basic questions of life and death. They wanted to know all about the gospel, heaven, and even hell. Their questions were not peripheral or sophisticated, but basic and elementary. The image they reflected was precisely what we have been discussing.

When an opportunity, then, awaits the Christian who, assured of God's power to work mightily today, dedicates his time and talents to communicating the gospel to 20th Century Man! With his interest in the basic facts of existence, the conservative Christian is in a position to offer what no one else can: a self-consistent and coherent system of truth that explains existence from start to finish. Christianity is, at heart, a religion based on historical fact. The gospel message, in both of its main points, is itself historical and factual. Christ's sacrificial death and bodily resurrection are matters that pertain to time and space. True Christianity offers no super-historical dodge. There is no blind faith in a "totally other" god who is unknowable. Instead there are documentary records concerning the God who made Himself known to various men throughout history, and supremely manifested Himself in human history in the Incarnation of Christ. Thus it is clear that conditions for highly successful communication between 20th Century Man and the Christian church now exist. The need and desire of the former is keen. The deposit of data in the Scriptures is exactly suited to meet these. Why, then, doesn't communication take place?

It is too early to say that it will not. There are encouraging signs among conservatives that the church is not going to miss her opportunity, but will rise to the challenge. But time is slipping by, and every day is a day of opportunity lost. It may well be that the church will have to be violently awakened from her stupor. Jonah's experience should stand as a strong warning. Had he gone to Nineveh initially, he would have been spared his hectic ordeal. After all, he only ended up doing what he failed to do in the first place. But there is a more excellent way; the way of obedience to God's call when it *first* comes. Confronted with this challenge, you will have to determine how to answer it. With that answer may lie the hope of nations and churches.

Chapter Two
Knowing and Going

So far, I have described present conditions for successful communication between the church and 20th Century Man as nearly ideal, and posed the question: Why, then, doesn't communication take place?" I also noted that it is yet too early to say whether or not the church will rise to the challenge.

Earlier a basic cause for failure to communicate—the false belief that successful widespread communication in this age is impossible—was mentioned. To the contrary, I adduced biblical principles and contemporary evidence to show that exactly the opposite is true, and I issued a challenge to recognize the facts and catch the vision.

Let me assume (for the sake of our present discussion) that your faith in the possibility of communication has been restored and that you wish to accept my challenge. What must you do, and how should you do it? It is now possible for us to discuss other principles and techniques fundamental to successful communication with 20th Century Man, and other secondary causes of failure relating directly to them.

WHAT IS COMMUNICATION?

The word "communicate" stems from the Latin *communis*, meaning "common." The fundamental root idea is to make a message common to both the communicator and the communicatee. This original significance must not be lost, since it so clearly points up the central problem in all communication. The purpose of communication is to convey a message containing facts understood by the communicator through such appropriate media as will cause the recipient of the communication to be able to understand too, thereby enabling him to share in the facts in the same way that the communicator does.

The authors of one textbook on communication have defined it this way: "Communication is the art of getting your ideas into somebody else's head" (Davis, et al, Direct Communication [Boston: Heath, 1943], p. 16). Christians can accept that definition with a slight, but important, change that makes all the differences in the world. While understanding that ideas in one sense must become his before he can effectively communicate them to another, the Christian would say, "Communication is the art of getting God's ideas into somebody's head."

Of course, messages, in varying degrees of precision and accuracy can be conveyed by an amazing number of media. One can nudge, kick, or push as a means of communication. He may blow whistles, ring bells, strike gongs, or activate buzzers. He can shrug his shoulders, wink an eye, draw a diagram, light a flare, or raise a flag. Obviously, the possibilities are almost infinite.

Any stimulation of any one of the senses, especially if prearranged, under the proper circumstances, can become a means of communication.

How, then, may this subject be limited? The God who made *all* things for His glory, and gave us commands to subdue *all* for man's use in His service, has placed no limits upon the media that one may employ. "All things are lawful" is a principle that is surely applicable. Of course the qualifying principle of expediency always must accompany and regulate its application. But perhaps Christians have erred seriously in placing narrow limits upon the media of communication. Rather than inquire as to how the subject may be limited, it may be more profitable to consider how one's appreciation of the possibilities may be expanded. Broader horizons, not narrower, seem to be one of the requirements of our times. The world's communication has been more successful than that of churches largely because of the excellence of technique and the breadth of media it employs. This success is due directly to the fact that (unconsciously) the world has stumbled upon this biblical principle of subduing *all* things.

Generally speaking, most effective communication involving any detail is carried on by means of sights and sounds. Together these two are classified as *audio-visual* communication. Within these two large categories, *again* numberless subdivisions may be made. The two most familiar are the spoken and the written word. While recognizing—and reemphasizing—that communication for Christians must not stop there, for present purposes, the discussion must be confined to the former classification. Even that may be broken into various subclasses. But the spoken word, as understood here, means witnessing (personal evangelism) and preaching: that is, direct communication by word of mouth.

Such delimitation of the subject must not be thought to contain nothing applicable to other means of communication, such as teaching, tract writing, etc. On the contrary, most of the principles and many techniques used are of universal application.

It is possible to speak *about* communication, and fail to answer the important question: "What is the message that a Christian must communicate?" The answer is twofold: the gospel and the Christian faith. Actually, these are not distinct; the gospel is a part of the Christian faith. But the two immediate jobs of the church are evangelism and edification (salvation and sanctification). In the Great Commission, evangelism is expressed by the command, "Make disciples of all nations." Edification is enjoined in the precept, "Teaching them to observe all things." In evangelistic communication the gospel is announced to lost men and women for the purpose of bringing them to discipleship. But once this is achieved, communication does not cease. It has only begun. Edification, leading to the sanctification of the elect, is a lifelong process.

Our purpose is to focus on evangelistic communication (without suggesting that the related matter of edification is of less importance). To do so, we must finally identify the field of communication. That brings us to a full recognition of the topic under discussion: communication of the gospel to disillusioned and lost 20th Century Man by means of witnessing and preaching.

Someone right now is thinking, "Why didn't you say so in the first place?" That would have been one possible approach. But it is of value to see something of the whole picture. It is too easy to forget the forest for the trees.

Having thus delimited the field, let us consider the what of evangelistic communication. There is a Christian *kerygma* ("message" or "thing preached"). It is a definite *deposit* of factual material (cf. II Tim. I: 12, 14).

Christians themselves must fully understand the message before they can successfully communicate it to others. Clarity of output is directly proportionate to clarity of intake. Moreover, the message must become personal and vital to the communicator. Christians convey the message through their personalities. They are not recording machines that merely play back exactly what is put on the tape. When they write or speak, they contribute something to the message—their own *understanding* of the communication. They express something of personal conviction, urgency, and enthusiasm. And they select terminology and style that they think will best convey it to their listeners.

It is vital, therefore, for Christians to understand both the facts and the implications of the gospel since it is the gospel that they must communicate.

In 1 Corinthians 15, Paul summarizes the good news:

> *Now I want to remind you, brothers, of the good news that I announced to you ... through which also you are saved ... that Christ died for our sins in agreement with the Scriptures; and that He was buried, and that He was raised on the third day in agreement with the Scriptures (The Christian Counselor's New Testament).*

Paul is explicit. The gospel consists of two points:
1. Christ's substitutionary death.
2. His bodily resurrection from the grave.

The book of Acts faithfully records examples of apostolic evangelistic communication. And in *every* instance where enough of the words are preserved to give an indication of what was said, these same two points stand out (cf. Acts 2:23, 24; 3:13-15; 4:10; 5:29-32; 10:39-41; 13:28-33; 23:6; 26:23).

Paul preached first negatively, then positively. Self-satisfied people, who do not recognize their personal sin, need first to hear the bad news of sin and its consequences. Such people are not fazed by appeals to "accept Christ as Saviour," "come to Jesus," or "let Jesus come into your heart." In this day of Bible illiteracy, they cannot be expected to understand words like that. Moreover, these exhortations (apart from the two factual points mentioned previously) do not constitute the preaching of the gospel. Frequently, conservatives err in watering down the gospel communication to mere exhortation. The good news (gospel means good news) is fundamentally factual. It contains data to be believed, not actions to be performed. In addition, self-satisfied persons are rarely moved, even by clear-cut exhortations, to believe those facts. In order to interest them in the good news, Christians (like Paul) must show them their need for it. It is true, men today willingly acknowledge the world's evil and the tragic state of world affairs. That helps. However, John Smith often thinks differently when it comes to a specific question of his own personal sin. There, he often has a blind spot. Yet, in times like these, it is far easier to demonstrate his need than previously. He has no defense. John needs to be reminded that the difficulty with the world is nothing else but the sum total of trouble caused by individual trouble-makers, of which he is one.

It is, then, an essential part of gospel communication to emphasize the fact that "Christ died for our *sins*." However, sin must be explained in terms of common ground, not with a holier-than-thou attitude! Moreover, it must primarily be explained as disobedience to the law given by a holy and just God. As such, it is an offence against God Himself. Only secondarily should sin be described in terms of its social effects.

The principle of contrast is involved in all of this. Successful communicators in all fields have long recognized the necessity for dark backgrounds. Traffic communications along the road are posted on signs in contrasting colors. Stores frequently display precious gems or silverware by the contrast of light and dark. Artists make use of the principle. Even doctors realize its importance. People who avoid doctors' offices like the plague can be induced to see a physician with little difficulty if they can be persuaded that they have cancer. The darkness of their condition makes even a doctor seem bright by contrast (it even works for dentists!).

It is exactly so with sinners. They are otherwise uninterested in the good news. Jesus explained that those who think that they are well will not come to the physician. But once the Holy Spirit has convinced them of their sin and its terrible consequences (through the ministry of His Word), there is no great problem in getting them to listen enthusiastically to the gospel. The good news shines forth most beautifully against the dark backdrop of sin and judgment.

Successful communication, then, demands a ready (or better, readied) listener. As the etymology of the word shows, communication is two-sided. Interest must be aroused, need sensed, desire elicited, and personal decision urged. And as shown, the times are ripe for this.

Of course, the sovereign Spirit, who works when, where, and how He pleases must regenerate, and effectually call the sinner to Christ. While the human procedure just outlined seems to be the normal process by which

He ordinarily works, He is neither bound to use it nor is He limited to these means alone.

That the process of evangelical communication ultimately depends upon God's regenerative power is an encouraging factor. God will call all of His sheep. But this in no way lessens our responsibility; God has determined to use human agents in carrying out His purposes. He has chosen to use the "foolishness of preaching," and therefore Christians must speak!

Granted that you understand the *nature* of the communication and your duty to become a communicator of the good news; what comes next?

One answer is, "Surely not the unsaved sinner!" Too many Christians have adopted a substitute plan of communication, which has all but replaced the divine method. They expect to communicate *within* the church instead of *from* it. They hold evangelistic services and urge the unsaved to come. They then complain of apostasy and indifference when there is no response! And in it all, they salve their own consciences, believing that they have done their part. Thus, again, they fall back on the same old excuse for failure: the difficulty of these "hard" times. Now, I hope we have decisively exploded that one, once and for all!

But God did not direct us to hold church services and invite the unsaved to them. Evangelistic meetings are not necessarily wrong in themselves, but it is decidedly wrong to use them as a *substitute* for God's program.

Two biblical principles are basic:

1. The unsaved man is dead in trespasses and sin, and therefore totally unable to take any initiative in spiritual things. We must expect him not to want to come to church. Since he is "dead" to all spiritual values, these seem "dead"—dull and uninteresting—to him.
2. The corollary principle is God's instruction to the church to "go" (Matt. 28:19). He said *take* the gospel to the lost. They were not expected to come and get it. The initiative in salvation comes from God; the church must represent His initiative by *going*. One reason people do not understand "grace" is that they fail to see it in the church's methods of communication. The church in the New Testament is always pictured as the *base* of operations *from* which (not *within* which) evangelistic communication goes *out*. Look at the pages of the Gospels and Acts. Almost without exception, such communication was carried on *outside* congregational meetings:

see it in a chariot, on a hillside, in a home, in the market, at the temple, in a jail, along a road, etc. The congregational services were viewed primarily as meetings designed for edificational communication between unbelievers.[1] They were the recharging of the battery for use elsewhere.

The second New Testament principle, then, is: Go where the fish are. Conservative Christians too often are cloistered behind their walls, holed up inside the Christian bubble. The fact that they have allowed a program of invitation to be substituted for the aggressive biblical program of outreach is clearly indicative of this condition. Doubtless, behind this is the fact that such a program is easier. It demands less time and personal sacrifice. But why has the church allowed the easier way to prevail? A large share of the problem stems from the matter discussed previously—the lack of an Elijah spirit. The concept of aggressive Christianity is inconsistent with present-day crawl-inside-our-shell-ism. The two stand or fall together. Aggressive Christianity catches the biblical vision and moves out to achieve it. By nature, it is not ingrown or complacent. Only a sick church—one like so many congregations that we know today—could permit such a substitution. Only a church convinced that aggressive out-reaching communication is useless could settle for a come-to-me scheme in place of the biblical go-to-them program. The two go hand-in-glove with one another. The biblical program was designed for an aggressive church that believes in the possibilities of widespread evangelization.

One of the interesting and wonderful things about Christian truth is that it doesn't matter which end of a problem you tackle first. If you solve one aspect of it biblically, that sheds light upon the rest. So even if you are not yet quite convinced that today is the day of opportunity, in one sense it doesn't matter, so long as you accept the biblical principle of outreach. Seriously implement that program in place of its substitute, and you will begin to see the opportunities for yourselves. A taste *of* such evangelistic communication will lead to a belief *in* it.

---

[1] Unbelievers were allowed inside Christian meetings and sometimes converted (1 Cor. 7:23 ff.) This means that the gospel message was always presented as an essential part of whatever else was preached (and should be today).

Chapter Three
Form and Substance

I shall now turn to an important theological distinction. For lack of better terms we'll call it the form/substance distinction. This distinction must not he understood in the Aristotelian, (or, for that matter, in any other philosophical) sense.

When Paul wrote the words "all things to all men" (cf. 1 Cor. 10:33), he was dealing with one aspect of the question in relation to Christian communication. When he wrote," 'If any man preach any other gospel ... let him be accursed" (Gal. 1), he was concerned about the other aspect.

Communication might be much easier if it were unitary, but it is not; it is a two-strata question. Like the earth there is a layer of unchangeable bedrock, and then there is the shifting 18 inches or so upon which we live. The two layers may be called the form (the surface) and the substance (the bedrock) of communication. When Paul spoke of becoming all things to all men, he was thinking of form. That is, the shape of the communication. When he rigidly denied anyone—angels included—the right to alter the gospel, he was thinking of substance. The form/substance distinction in Christian communication pertains, on the one hand, to those bedrock truths and principles that are immutable and, on the other, to those perennial adjustments that various times, persons, and places require in order to convey the message most effectively.

The trick, of course, is in striking the proper biblical balance. Throughout her history, the church has vacillated between extremes. One is over-accommodation, in which substance is sacrificed to form. The other is the tendency to can-and-refrigerate the substance in an outmoded form out of a desire to preserve the substance.[2]

Various movements within Christendom may be classified fairly accurately by their success or failure to strike the proper balance. Liberalism has

---

2   Actually, this distorts and destroys it.

invariably been on the left, sacrificing substance for form. The one great *un*changing factor from 19th to 20th century liberalism has been its attitude toward revelation. In both of its phases (rationalistic and existential), the rejection of the Scriptures as an inerrant standard of faith and practice remains at the heart of the liberal error. The old modernism was a pure individualism, where "every man did that which was right in his own eyes." The more recent theology of crisis has emphasized the Christian community and the subjectively encountered Word within the word as man's standard.

In place of a bedrock, substantial deposit of factual and unchangeable truth, contemporary theologians have had nothing more to offer but the subjective experience of a super-historical encounter, which they call revelation. Thus, by making the substance of communication subjective, neoorthodoxy has eliminated the distinction itself; subjective experience is anything but bedrock. Nothing is more thoroughly shifting by nature. They have confounded topsoil with bedrock.

Romanism, on the contrary, has characteristically taken its place far to the right. (Today, there is a strong move in many quarters toward the other direction.) In an attempt to preserve substance, she has frozen form as well. Operating under deep-freeze thought-forms from medieval times, she has consistently insisted that men conform to her in form as well as substance.[3] She too has destroyed the distinction. She has mistaken bedrock for form (though the rock on which she is founded is not the biblical one).

Only conservative Christianity is able to strike the balance. At times, of course, she tends either to the right or to the left. But when true to her principles, she declares herself on the side of changeless substance in ever-changing form. She can neither accept Rome's changeless substance in changeless form, nor liberalism's changing substance in changing form. She avoids both their errors while retaining the truth of each. In this lies her God-given strength. It is a strength that makes meaningful communication feasible.

Why not apply this distinction to what is going on in this article? A little reflection will show that the discussion has largely been about substance thus far. The nature of the communication and the biblical principles under consideration have almost all pertained to substance. When pointing out the trends of our times, however, we flipped the coin. But we flipped

---

3 That is why modern protests within Romanism have been so reactionary.

it back again to find out what scriptural principles applied to such times. Until now, the discussion has concerned absolutes—principles derived from inscripturated revelation. These are primary and unchangeable. But there are secondary matters that have to do more with form than with substance. These pertain to such matters as the scientific, educational, cultural, and literary aspects of communication. What we know of these must be accepted as provisional. Such information is useful insofar as it is accurate and, therefore, better enables the church to communicate. But since these data consist of suggestions from our times, for use in our times, Christians acknowledge that they are subject to error and to change. There is, to be sure, a thin line between them at certain points, and even some overlapping. That is to say, the church may not recognize a biblical principle until it is accidentally unearthed by someone in another discipline. Then, it becomes plain that God, in His dealings with men, used it from the beginning. However, one must be careful not to read into Scripture what is not really there. It is dangerous to declare the Bible on the side of contemporary scientific theories. Far too often, just that has been done.

Since the two extremes of over-accommodation and status-quo-ism both must be avoided, it is important to know how to do so. No better solution can be offered than a variation on the same theme: an aggressive, witnessing church is the only real insurance. How? you may ask.

The refrigeration of form grows largely out of fear: fear of change itself. It is the fear of a very real danger—that in changing form the substance might be impaired. Ironclad, and stereotyped ideas of *how* the message shall be communicated are clamped upon it. Soon, these become tradition. After that, because of their hoary age, they cannot be tampered with or even questioned—they are sacrosanct. Indeed, they become indistinguishable from the substance. But when they do, they bring about the very thing that everyone wanted to avoid—the substance is changed. It is changed by adding form that is mistaken for substance.

If there is one thing that does not characterize aggressive churches, it is fear. They see a job to be done and believe it can be done. They cannot be bothered about tradition. They are out on the battlefield doing the job, and whether new or old, they soon discover and use the techniques that work. Here, there is always the danger of pragmatism and the use of unethical means to reach noble ends. Not all conservative churches have avoided the danger.

Non-aggressive churches (and Christians), safely sheltered from the world, soon move out of touch with the times. Forms successfully used by their fathers, at a time when the church was still aggressive, are carefully perpetuated. Their children remember how effectively these once worked. But they have failed to recognize that times have changed. The old techniques prove effective no longer and should be replaced by new ones suitable to the new moods, attitudes, and problems of new times. Yet, when the old forms of communication fail, the blame is conveniently placed upon the difficulty and apostasy of the times. This conclusion leads to more discouragement, greater withdrawal, and even further refrigeration of technique. Only the grace of God can crack the ice that this swirling circle produces. The twin dangers here are formalism and hypocrisy.

One might think that the aggressive church would quickly fall prey to the danger of over-accommodation, since in her zeal to reach the lost she is willing to become "all things to all men." But this is rarely the case. Vital evangelistic contact with the world tends to sharpen theology. One's beliefs are continually on trial. He finds that he must be "ready to give an answer for the hope that is within him" at all times. Frequently, he is stumped. This drives him more deeply into the Book. His Bible study and prayer life are no longer academic, but living, throbbing with everyday interest and relevancy.

Churches that no longer believe effective witness is possible become ingrown. They take interest in the substance of Christianity only for its own sake. Study often becomes pedantic and trivial. Polemics replaces apologetics. Cold, sterile orthodoxy frequently results. Without knowing it, such churches, thinking they are bastions of truth, in time actually become more susceptible to heresy and unbelief. Spiritual muscles become flabby from lack of exercise. The spirit of the world imperceptibly creeps in, and with it, the subtlest forms of error and unbelief. Aggressive Christian communication is, therefore, very essential to the church.

While the church must be flexible in adjusting to new forms of communication, she must guard against molding the substance by the form. We have said that aggressive communication will largely solve this problem. But it cannot do everything. An intelligent understanding of the problem is also necessary.

Form exists for substance, not the reverse. This is an important principle to remember. The function of form is to contain and convey the substance. Thus, the goal is to achieve an *integration* between form and substance. Only then can there be continuity between the thought-forms of the day and the form in which the true communication is conveyed to minds that think that way.

But while a certain amount of *continuity* is essential, it cannot be *total*. There must be *dis*continuity also. The discontinuity pertains not only to substance (where it is often most striking) but to form as well. Aggressive Christianity changes both the thought and the thought-forms of others. What a tremendous effect a true national or international revival of religion would have upon contemporary thought-forms! The very language of our streets, our news media, and our businesses would be transformed. Christianity thus conforms to the thought-forms of society in order to *trans*form them. The relation with respect to form is, therefore, reciprocal. There is a borrowing and a contribution. The borrowing is consciously done in such a way that substance is not jeopardized and so that the contribution can be made. Thus, even in form, the communication of the church is not merely an echo, but also a voice.

Let us take a specific example: Contemporary society is biblically and theologically illiterate. The great words of Christianity like salvation, grace, justification, etc., for all intents and purposes, are useless in themselves in initial forms of evangelistic communication. Shall the church give up these words? Shall she adopt a new vocabulary based, for instance, upon present-day psychology? After all, today, people probably understand (or *think* they do) more complex psychological terms than religious terms. Should we translate Christianity into such modern terminology?

The answer is yes and no. Obviously, evangelistic communication must be lodged most entirely in *contemporary* language. Preachers' patter and pietistic jargon are strictly taboo. Effective communicators soon learn to dispense with "dearly beloveds" and "blesseds." The New Testament was written in *Koine* (fish-market) Greek, not in some literary form from the past. *Koine* Greek was the common language of the day. There must be continuity. But discontinuity is essential too. We cannot give up the basic terms of gospel communication simply because people don't understand them. Modern psychology, like other areas of society, simply does not have words that can be substituted for words like *sin, hell, judgment, faith,* and *repentance*. They must be retained. Experience shows, however, that these *essential* words are few.

What, then, is to be done? Simply this. In *contemporary* language, one must arouse interest in the communication. Then, only such technical Christian terms as are absolutely necessary may be introduced. And, these may never be used without careful explanation, definition, or illustration. Technical terms are of great value. If used in a gathering where they are understood, they help communication. They are more precise and save time. But when not comprehended, when used without explanation or in great profusion, they do nothing more than muddle and confuse. The crucial point is this: everything (these terms, and their meanings) must be explained in *contemporary language-forms*. The unknown must be made known by using the well-known.

This means that, in evangelistic communication, a certain amount of *instruction* is necessary. The safest rule is to assume that the listener knows *nothing* about the subject. Wise communicators, therefore, never use Christian shoptalk that to the outsider is merely jargon. Instead, like the psychologists and others who have successfully promoted public understanding of new words, Christians must sell the basic Christian terms all over again to this new generation. But selling can be done only in language that people already can understand. Failure to follow this rule accounts for a good deal of the ineffectiveness of the church in our time.

Listen to two examples of conservative Christian communication. The first demonstrates what I mean by outmoded form and unexplained technical terms received as unintelligible jargon. The second is a good example of relevant Christian communication. Both were directed to the unsaved public in general. Here is the first (italicized words indicate problem-words for unbelievers):

> "Except ye repent, ye shall all likewise perish" (Luke 13:3). These were the words of the *incarnate* Son of God. They have never been cancelled, nor will they be as long as this world lasts. *Repentance* is absolutely necessary if the *sinner* is to "*make peace*" with God" (Isa. 27:5), for *repentance* is throwing down the weapons of rebellion against Him. Repentance does not save, yet no sinner ever was or ever will be saved without it. None but Christ saves, but an *impenitent heart* cannot *receive* Him.

A sinner cannot truly believe until he *repents*. This is clear from the words of Christ concerning His *forerunner*, "*Repented* not afterward that ye might believe him," (Matt. 21:32). It is also evident from His clarion call in Mark 1:15, "*Repent ye*, and believe the gospel." This is why the apostle Paul testified "*Repentance* toward God, and *faith* toward our Lord Jesus Christ" (Acts 20:21). Make no mistake on this point, *dear reader*, God "now commandeth all men everywhere to *repent*" (Acts 17:30).

... In true *repentance* the *heart* turns to God and acknowledges: my heart has been set upon a vain world, which could not meet the needs of my soul; I forsook Thee, the *Fountain of living waters*, and turned unto broken *cisterns* which held none: I now own and *bewail* my folly. But more, it says: I have been a disloyal and rebellious creature, but I will be so no longer. I now desire and determine with all my might to serve and obey Thee as my only Lord. I *betake myself* to Thee as my present *Portion*.

Reader, *be you* a *professing* Christian *or no*, it is REPENT or PERISH. For every one of us, church-members or otherwise, it is either *TURN* or BURN—turn from your course of self-will and self-pleasing; turn *in brokenness of heart* unto God, seeking His mercy in Christ; turn with full purpose of *heart* to please and serve HIM: or, be tormented day and night, forever and ever, in the *Lake of Fire*. Which shall it be?" *Oh* get down on your knees right now and beg God to give you the spirit of true *repentance*.

What is wrong? First of all, too many technical terms are used entirely without explanation. Listen to these: *repent, incarnate, make peace with God, save, sinner, forerunner, brokenness of heart*. Now all these words and phrases are basic vocabulary—for a Christian, but not for the unbeliever. If you didn't have any trouble with them, ask yourself whether you may have become so accustomed to them that they did not strike you as technical terms at all. In addition, listen to the pietistic and outdated modes in which the appeal is presented: *Dear reader, I bewail my folly, I betake myself to Thee, be you ... or no, Oh get down on your knees*. People simply do not "betake" themselves any longer, or address others as "dear reader." That sort of language turns contemporary readers off!

Contrast a second communication on the very same subject.

REMORSE OR REPENTANCE

We are all great sinners, no better than Judas and Peter, and in some respects perhaps even worse. But how do we feel about our sin? And what do we do about it? If we feel nothing but remorse, we are like Judas, and that can lead to suicide, in one way or another: physically or spiritually, or both. For remorse is really no more than self-accusation, which can easily become self-pity, and then selfdestruction. But if we are truly repentant, we are like Peter, and that will certainly lead to salvation. For repentance begs for mercy and seeks forgiveness, while forsaking the sin and returning to God. The remorseful sinner feels sorry for what he has done to himself. The repentant sinner feels sorry for what he has done to God.

Do we still know the difference between remorse and repentance in this world? Do we still know how to weep about our sins? Well, many people don't even feel remorse, to say nothing of true repentance. They are worse than Judas.

A few years ago, a study was made of delinquent boys who were being held in police custody. They were all asked this question: "Why are you here?" Almost invariably the answer was: "Because the cops railroaded me," or "Because I didn't plan my getaway well enough," or "Because somebody ratted on me."

What does this tell us about our modern attitude toward sin? Is it a sign of the times? Are these boys only reflecting what they have learned from their elders? We live in a society that has real regret, no sorrow for sin. In fact, the great sin is getting caught. They may lament their stupidity but not their wickedness.

Doesn't that point to a very popular notion we have about our misdeeds? A thing is good if you can get by with it; it is bad only if you don't. Cheating in school, dishonesty in business, infidelity in marriage, hatred and violence and cruelty, drunkenness and vice and dissipation-these things and many others like them are considered to be bad, but they don't make us feel bad unless we get caught, unless they hurt us, unless we have to pay for them. And then we feel bad only because of what they do to us, not because of what they do to God. We don't like the consequences, but the deeds themselves don't bother us too much.

> Dr. Werhner von Braun has something to say to us about sin in this modern world, and it is interesting to hear him say it because he says it as a scientist who has been prominent in scientific developments during the space age ...

Is there not a great difference? Not one word; not one aspect of that excerpt is unintelligible. The subject "Remorse or Repentance" is a difficult one to present to the modern world which has lost not only its understanding of true repentance but even its capacity for remorse. The former communicator does not recognize the problem at all. The latter does. Therefore, he carefully explains the difference between repentance and remorse, defining and describing each and showing how they relate to modern man. It is cast in a modern mode. Illustrations are fresh and timely. Juvenile delinquency is mentioned; von Braun is quoted. The present-day problem with respect to repentance is therefore recognized, discussed, and satisfactorily met head-on.

In conclusion, carefully consider Henry Zylstra's plea for vital language:

> The plea for a more vital language in our preaching and apology arises from time to time among us. It is a plea which is ignored by some as a matter of no consequence, feared by some, too, as a threat to orthodoxy, and welcomed by others as an important and legitimate concern. Those who ignore the call for vitality in the diction, language, or style of our spoken and written word are, it seems to me, making a mistake. What they have at the back of their minds is probably something like this: the important thing is the truth, the whole truth, and nothing but the truth. That, they feel, is the main thing, and they go on to imply that the form in which that truth is uttered is neither here nor there really. The content, the idea, the substance is what matters. To talk about the language of such content, the style of such substance, seems to them like talking about the paper on which a king's message is written.
>
> All the same, such separation of truth from statement, of content from form, of idea from style, is a false and fatal separation. The form is essential to the meaning, to the understanding of it, and to the communication of it. The thing we have to say is inert, dead, and incommunicable until it becomes significant, gets its sign, assumes form, like the chaos of Genesis. It is void.
>
> Some have called language the dress in which thought is garbed. The

figure is mechanical, and it does not go far enough. Language is not so much the dress as the incarnation of the thought. The word is truth become flesh. Language is the body of the idea, and it is only in the body that we can become aware of it. When this body of the language fits the soul of the thought, it is characteristically expressive of that soul. This is what Buffon over-stated when he said, "The style is the man."[4]

---

4   Henry Zylstra, *A Testament of Vision*, pp. 70-71.

Chapter Four
Do It Well

The previous chapters dealt primarily with the substance of communication; what follows picks up where chapter three ends and pertains almost exclusively to form. Substance concerns the absolute, form the relative. The absolute is unchangeable and relies upon divine principles drawn from special revelation. Form relies upon contemporary moods and techniques, and is changeable.

However, as Zylstra indicated, form must not be thought unimportant. It is the vehicle by which the substance is conveyed. We who believe in the inspiration and inerrancy of the Scriptures recognize that precision of meaning depends upon precision of terminology and expression. Therefore, we see in the modes of communication, and their use, the potential for good or for evil. Form can make or break communication; it can muddle or manifest the message.

Since all communication is a matter of substance and form, we cannot escape the problem. Substance cannot be conveyed but in some form. Form may be thoughtless or careless, but nonetheless it is form. Therefore, since we cannot escape form, we must make the most of it.

First, let us note that the best of modern scientific technology should be employed to the full. Public address systems,[1] radio, film, television, tape recordings, and a host of other devices may be used in a variety of ways to help convey the message.

The two important things to discuss here under form are, again, the quality of these instruments and the way in which they are used. Poor video, for instance, compositionally or technically unsound, is worse than no video. Their form conveys an unwanted message that distorts the true one: Christians can't be very serious about what they are saying in such films, or

---

1   I know of one church that constantly has problems with its P.A. equipment, but goes on disrupting communication because it will not purchase an adequate system.

so it appears. Form-wise, Hollywood turns out some superior films. Christians cannot afford to do less. In fact, they should do *better*. They produce not merely for mercenary purposes, but for God's glory and the salvation of men. Christians simply cannot afford to do a half-baked job in the name of Christ. Good form calls no attention to itself; rather, it is so appropriate to the substance at every point that nothing but the message comes through.

The same must hold true of church architecture, and a number of other areas which, in their outward expression to the unsaved world, often say more to them than all the words we write or speak. Churches with unkept lawns, dingy paint, cheap (or gaudy) signs are decided hindrances to successful communication.

It is so easy to err in this realm. Good equipment, good buildings, and good maintenance all cost money. The subtle thing is that there are always ways to cut corners. Someone offers a less expensive model, which almost always appeals (and is bought), but also turns out to be less effective as well.

In those matters that pertain even remotely to evangelistic communication, the rule always must be that what the church offers is at least as good as the best the world has—and if possible, even better. This requires money. But Christian leaders must train the church that communication is *fundamental* to all the church does; therefore, communication can never be second-rate. We dare not distort the gospel message or lose opportunities to communicate because of misunderstandings about this or as a result of outright stinginess. The most wonderful message in the world must be sent in appropriate wrappings.

But the best equipment alone will not do the job; carefully trained personnel who prepare well to use it, and who keep it in good repair are also essential. A man who doesn't know how to run it can fumble around with the finest sound equipment money can buy, and turn an otherwise effective presentation into a ludicrous spectacle. A religious radio program at the most advantageous spot in the daily schedule, with the best adjacencies, broadcast over the most up-to-date facilities, can be turned into an amateurish farce by a preacher who doesn't use the medium properly. All the professional equipment and know-how will mean absolutely nothing if the speaker or his programming is unprepared, or if he himself lacks adequate appreciation of the problems, techniques, and possibilities of radio. Thus, the crucial principle governing this aspect of form is good use of good equipment for the glory of God. Improper use of good equipment, like the fair woman without discretion, is also a "jewel of gold in a swine's snout" (Prov. 11:22).

"But no one is perfect," you say. And you are correct. Everyone fails sometime. People rarely measure up to their expectations, let alone their full capabilities. What does God expect then? At least these things:

1. Careful consideration of one's own abilities and potentials so that he may choose the area of Christian communication in which he is likely to be most effective (speaking, working with equipment, personal one-on-one contact, etc.).
2. Willingness to serve happily in that capacity, whether or not it is the most attractive to him.
3. Desire to acquire all the training and skills available to enable him to do the finest job he can.
4. Flexibility and openness that allow objective self-criticism and improvement.
5. And, above all, the proper motives toward God in all he does, accompanied by submission to His revelation and providence.

How does one learn to communicate effectively? In the same ways he learns in any other field of endeavor. How does an artist learn to paint? He studies theory, but that is just the beginning. An artist will never learn to paint from books alone. Primary, in his training, is the study of paintings. He carefully analyzes good paintings to see what makes them good. He learns all he can of other artists' methods and studies their results in actual productions. He studies poor paintings as well and discovers what made them poor. He observes artists doing painting and asks them questions. All the while, he too is painting, trying to put into practice the good principles he has learned and to avoid the mistakes. And, he paints under supervision so that he doesn't learn wrong practices from the outset. Then, he paints, paints, and paints—on his own. Eventually, after much study and practice, he acquires a style of his own, based upon his experience and knowledge. Then, he teaches others.

Apply this to preaching, for instance. How few conservative ministers take preaching as seriously as artists do painting! How few have studied the sermons and methods of great preachers to any large extent. Still fewer ever watch a good preacher prepare his messages or have proper supervision of their own early efforts. Seminaries often lay greater stress upon substance than form. Practical theology is frequently minimized, or taught by persons who themselves may know how to preach but who do not know how to teach others to do so. A good football player doesn't always make a good coach. In seminary, student interests are consumed by theology, languages, exegesis, church history, and apologetics. Homiletics, counseling, and kindred subjects often are regarded as necessary evils for which only a very small amount of time can be spared. Poor curricula encourage students to look upon homiletics as an incidental. Yet, the practical department of a seminary represents the department concerned with communication. Rather than incidental, we must get students (and their professors) to see that practical studies are those courses that concern the use of the media which integrate and express the substance taught in the rest of the seminary curriculum. Both students and faculty must acknowledge this and take a deeper interest in the role of practical theology. Otherwise, in the ministry, substance will be sacrificed because of bad form.

How tragic it is to talk to young ministers, now in the pastorate, who suddenly awaken to the importance of the practical studies that they neglected (and often were encouraged to neglect) while they were in the seminary, and which (they now know) were not adequate anyway. The freshly-graduated minister usually flounders about—sometimes for years—until (in the hard way) he gradually develops second-rate, hit-ormiss methods of communication on his own.

The seminary student must learn how to communicate. This is one of the great imperatives of our day. The church that ordains students who graduate from a seminary with inadequate practical training runs the danger of growing apostasy among its ministry. Men ill-prepared to communicate the substance they believe, grope about, trying to communicate to the world and the church. When they fail, they may begin to wonder about the validity of the substance itself.

Karl Barth is an illustration of the fact that poor practical training leads to poor theology. He testifies to this himself:

> Once in the ministry, I found myself growing away from these theological habits of thought and being forced back at every point more and more upon the specific minister's problem, the sermon. I sought to find my way between the problem of human life on the one hand and the content of the Bible on the other (*The Word of God and The Word of Man*, p. 100).

Barth came to the conclusion that theology was not a solution, but only a description of human problems.

Commenting on the genesis of the dialectical theology, Hugh Ross Mackintosh says of Barth:

> It is no accident that this theology has ties with preaching; like that of others in association with whom his systematic work began, it sprang out of the felt mysteries and perplexities of the preacher's task (*Types of Modern Theology* [New York: Scribner, 1937], pp. 271, 272).

Barth's basic problem was one of communication. He cries out,

> The word of God on the lips of man is an impossibility .... As ministers we ought to speak the word of God. We are human, however, and so cannot speak of God" (*The Word of God and the Word of Man*, pp. 124, 186).

Perhaps the greatest impact of our day could come through the training of a new generation of orthodox ministers, who are *particularly well equipped in practical theology*, and who recognize the deep philosophical and dogmatic implications of form.

One of the tragedies of these times is that liberal seminaries and students do recognize the importance of effective communication, and are giving themselves wholeheartedly to its pursuit. We must outstrip them. If they work hard at communicating what they have to offer, how can we do less when we have the glorious gospel of the Lord Jesus Christ?

Now, let me make several observations and consider some principles concerning form, all of which seem important in themselves. They, therefore, are not necessarily related. While many methods of communication might be discussed with profit, discussion of these may be found everywhere. May I take the liberty to suggest the possibility of one method about which virtually nothing is being said or done today? I refer to debate.

Debate is a biblical method. Paul frequently reasoned or debated in the marketplaces (the public forum). He debated on Mars Hill. He debated in the synagogues.

In years past, Christians frequently used this method in preparation for ministry[2] and in the propagation of the truth. Recently, it has fallen by the wayside.

---

2   There are few better methods of teaching one to prepare well and become concerned about adequate substance presented in carefully thought-through form.

There is, however, one group—the self-styled Churches of Christ—which still employs the method, with great success. Their church was born in debate and has grown—amazingly so—largely through this medium. Stemming from that accomplished debater Alexander Campbell, in a few more than one hundred years, the Churches of Christ now claim over 14,000 congregations, many schools, missions, printing establishments, and national radio and TV programs. They have proven debate's effectiveness today.

Debate, through television, in the political and international realms, has gained in popularity in recent years. There is serious question whether *public* interest in debate ever ceased. May not conservatives resurrect this interesting tool as a valuable means of communication today? The thought, it seems, is worth mentioning. Perhaps someone reading this might catch the vision.

Of course, the form that such debate will take must be the highest. Respect for one's opponent, fairness, accuracy, winsomeness, and clear-cut logic must, of necessity, characterize any such new movement. New formats may be proposed. Liberal theologians, atheistic leaders, cultists. Romanists and others might be challenged by men well-prepared to defend and aggressively propagate the truth. The Chicago Conference on Inerrancy (1978) has called for aggressive action; is debate not a choice method for propagating biblical inerrancy?

The study of sociological problems and tendencies offers great promise. Take one example. Great changes are taking place in the social status of women here in America, but especially in Eastern countries. In many places they are just beginning to come into their own. This is a problem that should be of real interest to you, as it surely bears upon communication. It may open new opportunities and avenues for communication that heretofore did not exist. The ERA[3] is misrepresenting the Christian message. It could not get away with this if we were communicating that message clearly, convincingly, and in an interesting form.

Sociological studies may be of interest to those who communicate with specialized classes. Approaches to the poor, rich, or middle class will differ. Distinct problems, desires, viewpoints, and expressions demand variation. Children in the various age classifications all require specialized types of communication. Of course the deaf and mute, the blind, and the

---

3   Equal Rights Amendment

handicapped must be mentioned. Sociological and educational studies and techniques are therefore imperative.

In this shrunken world and shrinking universe, Christians are already confronted with the task of planning global, and perhaps in the not-too-distant future, interplanetary communication. Extensive space travel is a present possibility. The task of Christian missions in a few years conceivably could extend to communication with Earth colonies in other worlds. Even more difficult—and interesting—would be the question of Christian communication, if intelligent life were contacted in the planets. Interplanetary theology, of course, would dictate the necessity and basic principles of such communication.

But, apart from such speculation—which might not be quite as far-fetched as some may think—there is a very large, concrete job to be done right now. Large sections of mankind present a challenge to communication. Communism, Islam, and nationalism have been shutting the door to foreign ideological communication. New forms of spreading the gospel, in spite of deterrents, must be developed.

The world is in despair and lacks an ideology of hope with which to meet the challenge of these aggressive forces. Only conservative Christianity has such an ideology to offer. Here, I should suggest the possibility of debate again. Perhaps the answer lies in challenging the leaders of communism and Islam to public world-debate.[4] Nationalism, is of course, already being overcome by training nationals to return to and work among their own people. It is a huge task, but by the grace of God it can be accomplished. Christians must think in world terms, must give study and prayer to this matter, and work out means suited to *world* communication. Increasingly, there will be opportunities for Christians to transcend local and even national efforts.

Evangelism should be both occasional and stated. That is, Christians should be prepared to evangelize under all conditions and circumstances as the occasions arise. But they also should plan seasons, campaigns, and methods of evangelism. One of the most effective means of local evangelistic communication (of the planned sort) is house-to-house visitation. The principle for such evangelism is biblical (cf. Acts 20:20). It therefore belongs to the matter of substance. But the particular 20th century means that we employ are, to a large extent, a matter of form.

---

4   When was the last significant Christian/Islamic debate?

Two false substitutes sometimes sail under the colors of visitation evangelism. One is the "survey." In this method, the visitor is trying to find members of his own denomination, and the so-called "unchurched." The trouble is that at the end of the survey he knows very little more than he knew at the outset. Beforehand, he knew there would be people of all religions. Upon returning, his survey confirms this. He also knew, if he is a conservative Christian, that most of these are unsaved (whether churched or unchurched). Because of original sin, we should assume that every person is lost unless proven otherwise. So, from all the time and effort expended, how much did he learn from the survey that he didn't know already? And how much good did he do? How much evangelism took place? Usually, a survey involves a little more than a lot of wasted motion. Our concern is not whether one is churched or unchurched; we are concerned to know whether he is saved or unsaved.

Then, there is a second visitation substitute. It is akin to the first. We may call it "visitation invitation," but it is not visitation evangelism. The so-called "unchurched" are invited to church. But we have already discussed the error of a "'come-to-me" approach to evangelistic communication. In this technique, experience shows that all kinds of promises may be obtained, but very few solid results.[5]

The only approach that can honestly claim the name of visitation evangelism is one in which evangelism takes place. It will not be a mere survey, though records will be kept. It will not simply involve an invitation, though an invitation is extended at the proper time. It will be, first and foremost, evangelism, which involves some form of presentation of the gospel message. Nothing less is true evangelism.[6]

But evangelism must lead to edification. Therefore, this program—if biblical and successful—will be concerned first with the salvation of the householder, then with establishing him in a church where he may grow in grace. The invitation, then, is put where it belongs—after the evangelistic effort has been completed successfully.

Too frequently programs of this sort fail because of the attempt to reach as many houses as possible as quickly as possible. It is my contention that

---

5   One minister, using this method, visited 1,000 homes with the net result of one family won for Jesus Christ.
6   For a presentation of a full evangelism program, see *Shepherding God's Flock*.

the goal should be to reach as few houses as possible. What I mean is this: We should be geared to stay with a person as long as possible until he is won—and solidly in the church of Jesus Christ. Many evangelistic plans are superficial. They only skim the surface. People have questions, problems, and difficulties, which take time, prayer, and patience to solve. In other words, it takes in-depth communication. Yet, if at the first visit the householder is unresponsive to the gospel, Christians often shake the dust off their feet. It may be that the family circumstances, the problems at work, or any number of other things, temporarily caused disinterest. Why should we give up so quickly? What kind of communication is that?

It would be of value to discuss other areas of learning and knowledge, all of which, in their own way, have an effect upon Christian communication. But I shall not do so. It is of greater value here merely to suggest the sort of things that can make Christian communication more effective by mentioning the few examples I have given. This book was not intended to be exhaustive, but merely suggestive. If nothing else, I hope that I have opened new vistas to you and stirred you to think. I hope you will determine never to separate substance from form again. I urge you to work hard—in whatever way you may be communicating—to bring about a happy meeting of the two. I trust that your imagination has been challenged and your appetite aroused. I hope you will go further than I have. I hope that you will understand the important need for good communication in the life of the church. And, above all, I hope you clearly see the challenge and need for an aggressively communicating church to reach disillusioned 20th Century Man.

Sense Appeal and Storytelling

Sense Appeal and Storytelling[1]

The preacher was droning on about the Amalekites. And although he was only seven minutes into his sermon, all over the congregation heads began to nod, eyelids drooped, children began to squirm, and teenagers started passing notes. Then an amazing thing happened: suddenly, his audience snapped to attention. Young and old alike strained to hear. What had occurred? What was it that so abruptly transformed this apathetic group of parishioners into an alert, interested body? They came to life when they heard these words: "Let me tell you about an experience that I had during the last war ..." The preacher had begun to tell a story!

It hardly matters what age one is; so long as he can understand what is said, he will give rapt attention and almost immediate response to a well-told story. People with the most diverse interests and backgrounds will perk up when they hear that they are about to be treated to a story. Why is this? What is this near-mystical power that a story possesses? What is the appeal of a story? And what are some of the important implications of the story's attention-arousing and holding ability for Christian preaching? These, and others growing out of them, are matters that we shall examine in this essay.

The answers to the questions in the above paragraph are not hard to find, but the implications inherent in those answers are complex. For instance, it is true that we learn best what we see, touch, or hear and that, in discursive language, a story comes closest to the very experience of an event. Moreover, a story, well told, can go beyond the actual, omitting much that is irrelevant or that in real life may distract, while focusing on and emphasizing the major factors in the event. And, a story, by adding just those touches of detail and color that are calculated to inspire, entertain, inform, or stimulate a listener, can do what a reporter's abstract account cannot. In short, a good story is the creation (if fiction) or re-creation (if historical) of an event, or

---

[1] This essay first appeared in Logan, Samuel T. ed. *The Preacher and Preaching*, P&R Publishing, 1986. Used by permission.

series of events, tailored and told in a way best suited to achieve the purpose for which it is related.

Unlike a historical event, the story may be shaped and manipulated, and through it, the audience may be led to see in it whatever the storyteller wishes. Therein, of course, lies both its greatest potential and its greatest danger.

Please do not misunderstand; my use of the word *manipulate* here is entirely neutral. I do not want to imply, or wish for the reader to infer, that the narrator does anything wrong when he molds a story to serve his own ends, so long as he does not thereby misrepresent the truth. Among the advantages that the storyteller shares with the artist are the opportunities that their media offer for simplification, focus, and emphasis. The difference between didactic teaching and a story is like the difference between a photograph and a painting.

The flexibility the storyteller possesses becomes an ethical matter, involving the greatest responsibility. He may not use it to bend or twist the facts, either to lead others astray or even to convince them of the truth. Paul plainly denounced all such trickery in the cause of truth (1 Cor. 2:4, 5; 2 Cor. 1:12, 13; 1 Thess. 2:3, 4).

But it is equally true, when the storyteller has made his audience fully aware that he is about to do so, that he may exaggerate, underplay, take the listener on flights of fancy, etc., in order to make a point. The story is his to do with as he pleases—so long as he does not misrepresent what he is doing, and he uses the story in a way that may be judged moral by the most rigorous use of biblical standards.

Well-told stories also delight because, by them, one may so readily convey suspense, emotion, and surprise. The proper use of pause, inflection, voice, tone, quality, volume, pitch, rate, and bodily action all add to the effectiveness of communication in story form. When most effectively used, direct address, dialogue, well-chosen vocabulary, engaging style, and the like combine to produce what is perhaps the most powerful mode of human communication that exists. No wonder children and adults alike surface when a preacher moves from mere prose to portrayal.

Storytelling is the lifeblood of a message; stories can create and hold interest, make a truth clearer than the simple statement of a principle ever could, concretize abstract material, show how to implement biblical commands, and demonstrate how to make truth practical and memorable. No wonder Jesus used so many of them!

The preacher will do well to use them freely, too. But a precautionary explanation is in order at this point. I am not advocating the string-of-pearls method of preparation, according to which the construction of the preacher's message amounts to little more than a number of stories strung along a theme like the pearls of a necklace. In such cases, there is little or no exposition, and hardly any reasoning or grappling with truth. One *focuses* on stories rather than on the biblical passage. As a result, the preacher comes up with a sermon that looks very much like it could have been preached at the Marble Collegiate Church by Norman Vincent Peale.[2] No. We don't need that. Every sincere listener in the congregation should go away from a message knowing

1. What the passage (or group of passages) means; i.e., he should now understand it, even if he didn't before.
2. What the passage means to him; i.e., he should know what the Holy Spirit intended to do to him in the passage.
3. What he must do to obey any commands, appropriate any promises, etc., i.e., he should know how to convert the passage into life and ministry.
4. That the authority for what the preacher is teaching clearly comes from the Scriptures; i.e., he should be able to see that the preacher got what he is saying from the biblical preaching portion under consideration.

Plainly, if those four elements are necessary for preaching to be biblical (and they are), a sermon may not be only a string of stories—even if they are pearls. Indeed, stories ought to be properly used to help the preacher accomplish all four objectives, but stories cannot be substituted for even one of those objectives. Within the framework of those four elements, stories have not only a valid, but a valuable use.

There is much, then, to storytelling—much more than can be revealed here. But I shall describe some of the principal factors involved in storytelling, making an attempt to disclose a number of the secrets that for many have remained veiled far too long. But first a word about the title of this chapter.

---

2   Peale was a master storyteller and the preacher can learn something about storytelling (not about preaching content) from him.

The original title suggested for this chapter was "Vividness and Illustration." For several reasons, I prefer the present title. In the first place, while the word *vividness* has a long history among many homileticians, in my opinion, it has played a nefarious part in limiting thinking about the appeal to the senses to one sense alone—the sense of sight. In fact, the possibilities in preaching are much greater. All of the senses—taste, hearing, touch, smell, as well as sight—are fair game for the preacher. I preferred, therefore, to replace the word *vividness* with the two words *sense appeal*.

In the second place, the word *illustration* too shows the very same narrow tendency to confine sense appeal in storytelling to sight (to "illustrate," of course, is to "light up" or "make bright"). Since, through greater use, its etymological coating has worn much thinner than the one in which "vividness" is encased, it might be safe to use it to cover every sort of sense appeal in preaching. But there is already another better word available: sto*rytelling*. Because it is so much better, I have determined to use it instead.

You will have noticed, naturally, that I began the chapter with a short story about storytelling in preaching. I have already said quite a bit about storytelling, but virtually nothing about sense appeal. Because the latter is the broader of the two topics, I shall begin with it.

Sense Appeal in Preaching

By sense appeal, I refer to the preacher's audio-visual appeal to the five senses.[3] Through sense appeal, the preacher is able to help his audience "see," "feel," or otherwise "experience" what he is talking about in a way that closely approximates the reality about which he is preaching. I say "closely approximates," and I put quotation marks around the words *see*, *feel*, and *experience*, because while sense appeal stimulates the senses in a way that *approximates* the reality, this arousal of the senses does not always correspond *exactly* to the arousal elicited by the event itself.

But in the successful use of sense appeal, there is a reality to what occurs: feelings are stimulated. The imagination (notice how this word also is restricted to the sense of sight—*imagination* is from *image*), or perhaps it is better to use a broader term, the *memory* is activated by the preacher's

---

3   It is important to recognize that, as television has taught us, congregations are not merely *listeners*, but also *viewers*.

evocative language so as to arouse the listener's senses and to enable him to "experience" the event about which he speaks.

Sense appeal, then, is concerned not merely with cognitive matters, but especially with those intellectual considerations that affect the emotions; it is essentially *emotional* appeal—an appeal that is successful only when it stirs the members of the congregation emotionally to experience what the preacher is speaking about. Thus, to *experience* something is more than to *hear about* it or even to *think about* it. It is an appeal that helps the listener/viewer to relive or, for the first time, to live through an event. It is the recall of an event, or the recall of aspects of old events stored in the memory, creatively reconstructed into a new experience pattern, together with all of the emotions appropriate to the event. The difference between merely thinking about something and experiencing it (unless thinking leads to experiencing, as it may and often does) is greater than the difference you see when watching a program on a black-and-white or a color television set. One of the reasons why poor preaching is dull is that the preacher himself fails to experience what he is talking about as he speaks—there is no joy, sense of awe, tingling down his spine, or whatever. When *he* fails to relive the event, it is almost axiomatic that his congregation will "experience" that failure. In preaching, it is not enough to talk *about* something; the preacher himself must experience it afresh.

So the major purpose of vividness, or sense appeal, is to add the dimension of reality to truth by helping the listener/viewer to live through or relive (experience) whatever the preacher is teaching.

There are many ways to appeal to the senses in preaching, but we shall consider three:
1. The use of sensuous (not sensual) or evocative language.
2. The appropriate use of sound.
3. The effective use of gesture.

To these, storytelling may be added, but I shall reserve a separate section for that discussion.

The Use of Evocative Language

Shout "fire!" in a crowded place, and people (who believe you) will think, feel, and act exactly as if the building were on fire, even if it is not. Language, skillfully chosen and used, has power. As the example shows, it has the power to produce the same effects as the actual event. It is clear, also, that context and manner are all important; it is a matter of *shouting*, in a *public place*, in a *convincing manner*, that gets the response.

Sometimes, however, the mere use of a word itself will elicit a desired (or undesired) response. Take, for example, Paul's use of the word *Gentiles* in Acts 22:21, 22. There was such hatred for Gentiles among these Jews, it seems, that they would not accept the idea that God had sent Paul to preach the gospel to the Gentiles. Indeed, when Paul introduced the subject, they would not even allow him to discuss the matter. In that case, the context—the kind of audience to which he spoke, with their racial prejudice—was the critical factor. Like fire in a fireworks factory, the word *Gentiles* among them was incendiary. Manner was an unimportant factor, while in the former incident, *how* one informed the public of the fire might have been altogether determinative of their response. Can you picture a crowd believing someone who, in a lackluster manner, casually announces, "Oh, by the way, I should tell you—this place is on fire"? Or how about someone who, as he shouts "fire!" is snickering and giggling? Or suppose there is no problem concerning the manner and the context, but the wording itself creates the difficulty: "I want you to know that this building may be on fire. I don't know this for a fact since I haven't seen any fire or smelled any smoke myself, but it is altogether possible because someone just told me so." That sort of hedging (typical of much preaching) sends a confusing message.

So you can readily see that communication—and evocative language as one type of it—is a matter of content, context, and manner. Emotions will be stirred, and action will be elicited only as all three are properly related to the congregation and the preacher.

While keeping these facts in mind, let us consider evocative language a bit more closely. What sort of language is it? It is the language of sense appeal, language aimed at the senses. But what sort of language is that? How does it differ from other language? What is peculiar to it?

With one group, the word *Gentiles* would not be evocative. That is to say, it might be used freely and factually without evoking any emotional response whatsoever. With the Jews mentioned in Acts 22, it was a highly evocative term. It is important, therefore, to recognize the fact that the same word used in one context, with one sort of audience, may be evocative, but when used elsewhere may not be. Learning to choose and use language, then, is not simply a matter of discovering which words are evocative and which are not; it involves other factors (such as context and tone of voice) as well. Indeed, given the proper conditions, it is possible to use almost any word evocatively, and likewise, it is possible to reduce or eliminate the evocative effects of any word. Therefore, it is essential for the preacher who wishes to use sense appeal successfully, not only to choose words that properly depict what he wishes to convey, but to become sensitive to how those words relate to times, places, persons, and contexts, etc., and to the manner and tone in which he uses them.

Now, while all of this is true, it is important to note that there is one sort of language that in itself especially tends to be evocative: language that by its very nature is sense-oriented. Picture words (green, *flashing*), onomatopoetic words *(buzz, bang)*, tactile terms *(prickly, soft)*, olfactory words *(rancid, fragrance)*, and terms that stimulate the taste buds *(sour, briny)* are words of this sort. Often, for full effect, these words must be used in combination with others: "the horror of eating green mashed potatoes," "a sinking feeling at the sight of that flashing red light in the rearview mirror," "as the saw buzzed through his plaster cast," "his finger was in the car door as it slammed shut with a bang," "a prickley burr stuck to my big toe," "I laid my aching head on a cool, soft pillow," "the dead animal smelled like rancid butter," "the evening air was heavy with the fragrance of rose blossoms," "it was worse than sucking on a sour lemon," "he rubbed briny pickle juice in the open wound."

As you can see, many feelings (not just those clearly indicated by the terms listed) are evoked by these brief clauses, even without a complete context. Consider also the sentences, "The chalk continually squeaked as he wrote on the chalkboard," and "She slowly rubbed her finger across the skin of the balloon." If you, like many people, feel a chill run up your back as you listen to the two actions described, chances are that this language *alone* can produce that chill. Read the sentences again; visualize and "hear" what is happening. Am I right? Apart from the act itself, merely imagining it can produce a chill. Of course, authors of erotic novels depend on this power of language to evoke sexual arousal in the reader. The world has learned to appeal to emotions for its sinful purposes; when will the Christian pastor learn to do so in order to present the truth in all its edifying reality and power?

The purpose of using evocative language in preaching is to help the members of a congregation experience the full reality of the truth and to enter into the event about which the preacher is speaking. The idea is not to change or enlarge what the preaching portion has to say, but to enable the listener/viewer to fully understand it. Some people can picture, feel, or otherwise experience what a sentence like this means merely by reading it:

> Now when they heard of the resurrection from the dead, some scoffed. (Acts 17:32a).

With their "mind's eye," they can "see" the scorn registered on the faces of these Greek philosophers to whom the resurrection was ludicrous, given their view of the body. With their mind's ear some people can "hear" the philosophers jeering and laughing among themselves. For most, however, the preacher will have to bring the scene to life for his listeners/viewers in order to draw them into the event. To do so, he will depend largely on evocative language. That is a part of *ministering* the Word.

The Appropriate Use of Sound

But language alone will not suffice. In expressing the philosophers' sneers, the preacher might appropriately expel his breath in a hissing sound like that which might have been emitted by the scoffers as they spoke contemptuously of "a resurrected body!" That is to say, the preacher himself will sneer as he speaks the words.

Sound! How important it is as one appeals to the senses. Pitch, rate, timbre (or quality), volume—all of these factors are of significance. Moreover, sounds themselves sometimes count more than words. A preacher is truly free in his preaching when he has reached the point where he can make sounds that cannot be found in the dictionary. There is an illustration that I use about a tin garbage can in which I express the fit of the lid on the can by the word "schunk!" Everyone who has punctured his finger with a needle will respond knowingly to the sound "ooooh!" And who doesn't know what "oof!" means when uttered by someone running into an open drawer stomach first? Such sounds and noises, when judiciously used, add immensely to vividness (or sense appeal) in a sermon. Yet, I venture to say that not more than one out of one hundred preachers who may read these lines uses them.

Let me suggest that the next time you listen to an effective communicator—perhaps a television storyteller—listen for nondictionary sounds and noises. You will understand better what I am talking about when you actually *hear* it. The better the preacher, the more freely and easily he uses sound; dull, poor preachers are afraid of sound. One sign of good preaching is a preacher's freedom to make meaningful sounds in the pulpit.

Of course, volume, rate, pitch, and quality are of great importance too. All of these should be governed by content and serve to make the content clear. Loud volume when speaking of love makes little sense in most contexts. Reading Matthew 23 without raising one's voice is equally bad. The sound should grow out of and be appropriate to the content at every point. Pitch and rate are automatically controlled by excitement and muscle tension. Quality, or voice timbre—whether melodious, growling, or shrill—also must conform to content. Content control is the central thing to be kept in mind.

But does one *consciously* "growl" or increase his speaking rate? Rarely. Such things come naturally, without conscious thought, to the seasoned preacher. He *focuses on what* he *wants* to *say*, not on *how* he is saying it. But all the while, he allows himself to enter into, relive, and experience the content. Doing so affects the muscle tension, which in turn automatically adjusts pitch, and to some extent, quality and rate. His body automatically adjusts to what it experiences. Of course, evocative language, well chosen beforehand during preparation, can help *him* to relive the experience, as well as his congregation.

But he can do more. And the novice *must* do more in order to develop such capacities. At other times, when he is out of the pulpit, he can *practice* choosing and using evocative language. Each day he can prepare to tell the story of something that took place during the day, carefully selecting the best possible evocative language that is appropriate to it. On the way home, he can practice telling it. Then, that evening, he can tell it to a dorm mate, to his wife, or to his family. In such a setting he can feel free to experiment with all sorts of accompanying sounds and gestures. If he does this regularly, for an extended period of time (six months), soon he will discover that what he has been doing consciously on weekdays will have an unconscious effect on his Sunday preaching without any special effort to think about the matter while delivering the sermon.[4]

---

4 Recordings, studied later, will demonstrate progress.

Of course, in sermon preparation, he will work on choosing evocative language too, and will be sure that his sermon outlines contain these choices. Soon, he will find it increasingly easier to make such selections. Before long, volume, rate, and pitch will begin to conform more and more to content. They are the product of learning to relive an event.

The Effective Use of Gesture

Language and sound are accompanied by gesture (here, I shall use the word to refer to any use of the body in communication, whether overt or covert) when preaching. The body communicates. Smiles or frowns, hand gestures, motion of the body—all are an essential part of sense appeal. When speaking of the "horror of eating green mashed potatoes," a smile would destroy the communication; a wincing grimace of the face would aid it. How can you speak about the "prickly burr" or the mashed "finger in the car door" without appropriate accompanying gestures? Closing the eyes and drawing a long, slow nasal breath would be most fitting when speaking about "air heavy with the fragrance of rose blossoms."

Hand gestures (as well as some other sorts of bodily gestures) may be classified in three categories: *emphatic* (e.g., slamming the fist on the pulpit while saying, "We will not give in to Satan!"), *indicative* (e.g., pointing while saying "that one, over there"), and *descriptive* (e.g., measuring from hand to hand while saying, "It was about that long").

Again, practicing gestures is profitable and ought to be done at times other than Sunday morning. Constant practice will pay off quickly. Uncomfortableness and awkwardness in using gestures can be overcome in only one way—the same way that the discomfort of learning how to skate is overcome: by persistence.

So, to speak of vividness, or sense appeal in preaching, is to speak of a complex matter. It is not merely a question of painting word pictures. There are four other senses to which one may appeal, and the means for doing so involve the whole person, including his language (style) and his delivery (use of voice and body). And all of these are controlled by content.

Storytelling

Storytelling, perhaps, has the widest appeal to listeners simply because it makes the greatest use of evocative language. Stories cannot be told without it. The two, therefore, go together.

There are fundamentally two kinds of stories: true and fictional. Of course, many may be a combination of both. These may come in both expanded or condensed forms. The expanded versions, parables, long examples, allegories, and just plain old stories are, properly speaking, stories. Examples and instances, on the other hand, are mini- and minuscule stories: they are shrunken or abbreviated stories.

Stories are constructed in various ways: as analogies, similes, metaphors, extended metaphors (allegories), extended similes (parables), etc. All forms may be used in preaching. The "I ams" of Jesus ("I am the Bread of Life," "Water of Life," "Light of the World," etc.) are little stories. These story-like ways of saying things all triggered a wealth of meaning to those who knew and appreciated the rich Old Testament background to which they allude. The mini-story, "I am the door," spoken against the background of the entire shepherdly imagery that accompanied it (cf. Ps. 23; John 10), was as much connotative as it was denotative.

So, one principle of storytelling is to be sure that the stories will evoke much from the background of the congregation to which it is told. Agricultural allusions in a rural church (when used accurately) would be more powerful than many narrowly urban references. Of course, a preacher must be sure-footed here; otherwise his choice may backfire. He'd better not speak of the momma, papa, and baby bull to farmers (in some urban congregations a number of persons wouldn't even catch the error)!

And, of course, the opposite principle also holds true: new, unique, and different materials evoke a response when *they are carefully described and explained.* The unknown can best be made known by means of the known. Frequently, new truth can best be communicated in story form.

A third principle of storytelling is to tell about something that is old and familiar in a new and different way. Look at it from a new angle. This is what Jesus did with His "I ams."

A fourth principle is to avoid canned, trite, worn stories. Find your own. Use your own experiences; refer to things around you. When Jesus said, "Consider the lilies of the field ..." doubtless He gestured with a sweep of the hand toward flowers that were growing all around them. All of creation is God's storybook—read it. Search it until you know all about it. A preacher must develop the capacity to use his senses if he wants to arouse the senses of others. He must become super-alive to the world in which he lives. The

God who redeemed us in Christ is also the Creator of the world. Because He is one, there is a correlation between the created world and the new creation in Christ. Everything in creation is in some way analogous to spiritual truth.

How does one go about learning to tell stories? I shall give you two suggestions. First, buy a notebook. As the first order of business every morning, when you enter your study, look around you and discover what is there (your initial problem will be to learn how to see, hear, smell, taste, and touch again those things you have learned ordinarily to overlook). Think about that wastebasket containing pages of crumpled, discarded thought—what could it mean? How could it be used to illustrate what truth? Stare at your telephone, that potential link that you have with nearly the entire world. Listen to the scratch of your pen on the paper as you write. Run your finger over the grains in the wood of your desk. Think about the scratch on it and how it got there. Take the cover off a magic marker and smell the ink ....

Why, there is enough material in that study alone to keep you in the illustration and storytelling business for several lifetimes! But you must learn to open your senses to it. Because through life we learn to ignore much that exists and much that is happening around us—which we must; otherwise we'd get little accomplished—we go through day after day missing much that could be turned into stories. The ignoring process that we have learned, preachers must learn to reverse. Daily effort will be required to do so.

Each day, in your notebook, write down at least one example, illustration, or some sort of story that you glean from your examination of the study alone. Do that every day for six to eight months. Don't be concerned about whether it is good or bad. Write it down, after prayer, before you do anything else. Soon, you will discover, you will sense more and more—more quickly—and stories will flow. Furthermore, they will get better and better; in time, it will become great fun.

The second suggestion is this: take your notebook into the church auditorium, and/ or anywhere else that you teach, and (every week) write down at least two more story plots from what your senses tell you is there. That practice will enable you to actually point to, or comment about, something around you in your sermons or talks during the coming weeks ("Do you see that light over there? Well ...," etc.).

Now the stories suggested above have to do with things. They are good, especially as brief touches (mini-stories) in a sermon. And they are easier to start with. But you will discover that the most effective stories you tell, like Christ's parables, are more extended stories that have to do with persons in action ("A sower went forth to sow ...") and/or in conversation (note the quotation marks in a modern translation). Dialog is very helpful in enabling the listener to enter into and live the story; it tends to make the events of the story occur at the very moment when it is being told. No wonder Christ used so much dialogue.

But how can you develop these stories involving persons in conversation and in action? Basically, in two ways:
1. By making up fictitious stories ("Suppose a farmer had just plowed his field ...").
2. By keeping your eyes and ears open wherever you are.

When others are relaxing, oblivious of all that is happening, a wise preacher is working. He is *always* looking, listening, searching for such material. If he will only keep awake, jotting down notes immediately so he won't forget, he will collect reams of good material in no time. And most of it will come to him; he won't have to go after it.

So, preacher, after you have worked hard regularly at these activities (daily) for some time, you will notice something interesting beginning to happen: *as you are preaching,* stories of all sorts will pop into your head out of the blue. Some of these will be good; most of those that come early on won't be so good. You will be wise, at first, therefore, not to trust yourself to use them on the spot, *but as soon as the sermon is over,* jot down a note on such story lines and revise them afterward if they show promise. You will find that you may want to use some of them later.

One reason for not using such stories during the sermon is that to tell a story effectively, you must think through the *very best way of wording* it. Is there a "punch line"? What should be its exact wording? What is the best sequence to use in telling it? These and other such questions should be considered.

But, at length, the time will come when, after having done this, even these processes will become largely automatic and, at last, you will be able to use many of these stories on *the spot, as they occur to you.* That is when preaching has become truly free. You will discover yourself writing material into your outline for the next time, things you never thought about until you delivered your sermon. But that stage comes only after much careful, disciplined effort of the sort I have already suggested.

Stories put windows in sermons through which people may see, hear, and smell. But you can never get your congregation to see or hear what you, yourself, have not first tasted and touched. So, above all else, take God's Word seriously enough to come fully alive to its truth and penetrate deeply enough into His creation to discover all the analogies you need. At length your preaching and your congregation will come alive too!

The extended story, as over against the story in mini-form, when complete, consists of five elements:
1. Background or introductory materials.
2. A complication (or problem), which causes
3. Suspense, leading to
4. The climax (or resolution of the problem), ending with
5. A conclusion.

These five elements may be diagrammed in their natural sequence as follows:

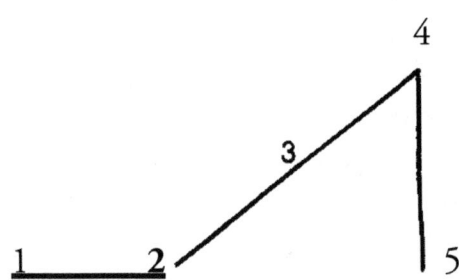

The diagram indicates three things:
1. The natural order of a story.
2. The length of time devoted to each element.
3. The level of interest sustained at each point.

The story's background begins on a normal, acceptable level of expectant interest, rises upon introduction of the problem (complication), and builds as suspense mounts. At the highest level of interest, the resolution (climax) occurs. Then, the interest level drops. That is why the conclusion must be brief (sometimes it is not needed at all; the climax and conclusion come together). Examine Christ's parables in the light of this diagram.

Much more could be said about sense appeal and storytelling, but this brief analysis, plus the practical suggestions introduced, ought to provide a considerable amount of help to those who are willing to earnestly consider and follow them in order to make truth memorable, clear, appealing, moving, applicable, and practical.

www.ingramcontent.com/pod-product-compliance
Lightning Source LLC
Chambersburg PA
CBHW060518100426
42743CB00009B/1365